THE SECOND PENGUIN BOOK OF CHRISTMAS CAROLS

ELIZABETH POSTON

Elizabeth Poston lives in Hertfordshire, where she was born. She was educated privately, at the Royal Academy of Music, and on the continent. During her post-student years she once found herself locked up with a goat in a mountain cell in southern Europe, but was released when she proved to be carrying not code but folk songs. She returned to England to accept the B.B.C.'s invitation to join their wartime staff, and fought a secret war among the 'Bushmen' of the European Service as musician-in-charge under Whitehall directive. She broadcast to North and South America, Australasia and the Near and Far East. After the war she resigned, to resume her own work, and acted as adviser at the inception of the Third Programme. She has travelled widely, distinguished herself in almost all fields of music, and covered an unusually wide ground creatively in the concert hall, theatre, films, radio and television, the church, youth and education, and the inspired nonsense of Hoffnung. Her publications include books for children, a modern hymnal and a work on France, as well as the first Penguin carol collection.

THE SECOND PENGUIN BOOK OF

CHRISTMAS CAROLS

COMPILED AND EDITED
WITH ARRANGEMENTS, NOTES,
TRANSCRIPTIONS,
AND AN INTRODUCTION BY
ELIZABETH POSTON

PENGUIN BOOKS

Penguin Books Ltd, Harmondsworth, Middlesex, England
Penguin Books, 625 Madison Avenue, New York, New York 10022, U.S.A.
Penguin Books Australia Ltd, Ringwood, Victoria, Australia
Penguin Books Canada Ltd, 2801 John Street, Markham, Ontario, Canada L3R 1B4
Penguin Books (N.Z.) Ltd, 182–190 Wairau Road, Auckland 10, New Zealand

—

First published 1970
Reprinted 1973, 1977

—

—

Made and printed in Great Britain by
Richard Clay (The Chaucer Press) Ltd, Bungay, Suffolk
Set in Monotype Times

CONTENTS

ACKNOWLEDGEMENTS

ACKNOWLEDGEMENTS are made for permission to use copyright material granted by the following copyright owners: the Archive of Folk Song, the Library of Congress, Washington, D.C., for *Joseph and Mary* (*The Cherry Tree Carol*), *Oh, Mary and the Baby, sweet lamb* and *The Twelve Days of Christmas*; J. J. Augustin Incorporated Publishers, New York, for *Sunny Bank* (*Christmas Day in the morning*) from the University of Virginia (Manuscript) Collection of Folk Music; *Shepherds in Judea* (*As shepherds in Jewry*); *A Virgin most pure*, tune and stanzas 1–5, cited in *Down-East Spirituals and Others* by George Pullen Jackson; Berea College (The Hutchins Library), Kentucky, for *Juda's Land*; Albert & Charles Boni Inc., New York, for the tune and first stanza of *Child of God* (*The little cradle rocks tonight in glory*), *Poor li'l Jesus* and *O Mary, where is your baby?* from *Mellows* by R. Emmett Kennedy; The Broadman Press, Nashville, Tennessee, for the reprint of *Shepherds, Rejoice* in *The Sacred Harp*, 1868; The Da Capo Press, New York, for the tune and stanza 1 reprint of *A Virgin most pure* and the tune *Perseverance* in Wyeth's *Repository of Sacred Music Part Second*, 1820; Dover Publications Inc., New York, for *Sweep, sweep and cleanse your floor* from *The Gift to be Simple*, by Edward D. Andrews; Duke University Press, Durham, North Carolina, for *Jesus born in Bethlehem* ('*Song of Jesus*') from the Frank C. Brown *Collection of North Carolina Folklore*; Helen Hartness Flanders for *Saint Stephen and Herod* from *Ballads Migrant in New England* by Helen Hartness Flanders and Marguerite Olney, Farrar, Straus & Young, New York; Hastings House, New York, for *Babe of Bethlehem* and *Come away to the skies* reprinted from *The Southern Harmony*, 1854; *The Journal of American Folklore* for *The Blessings of Mary* collected by Richard Chase (xlviii, 390, 1935), stanzas 2–5 of *Child of God* collected by Emma M. Backus (xii, 272, 1899), and the words of *Wasn't that a mighty day* collected by Anna Kranz Odum (xxvii, 264, 1924); The New York Times Company for stanzas 1–10 of *Baby born today* from *Folk-Songs of America* by Robert W. Gordon; Oak Publications, New York, for the reprint of *Rise up, shepherd, an' foller* and *Heav'n bell-a ring* from *Slave Songs of the United States*, 1867; Penn Community Services Inc., Frogmore, South Carolina, for the tune and stanza 1 of *Mary had a baby* from *St Helena Island Spirituals* collected by N. G. J. Ballanta-Taylor; Theodore Presser Co. (Merion Music Inc.) for Charles Ives's carol: *Little Star of Bethlehem*; G. Schirmer Inc., for the following four songs collected by John Jacob Niles: *Down in yon forest* and *Lulle Lullay* from *Ten Christmas Carols from the Appalachian Mountains*; *I wonder as I wander* from *Songs of the Hill-Folk*; *Virgin Mary, meek and mild* from *Seven Negro Exaltations*.

I wish to express my thanks to Mr Alan Jabbour, Head of the Archive of Folk Song and his staff, the Library of Congress; Mrs Ruth Noyes and Mr David

Bland, successively Librarians of the Vaughan Williams Memorial Library, the English Folk Dance and Song Society, Cecil Sharp House; the Librarians and staffs of Central Reference Library and Central Music Library of the B.B.C.; the Hertfordshire County Library; the London Library; Dr Alicia Percival and the D. M. S. Watson Library, University College, University of London; the British Museum; Mr Ashbel G. Brice, Director of Duke University Press; Dr W. R. Reed and Miss Muriel Smith; and friends on both sides of the Atlantic, too many to mention, who have helped in the preparation of this book.

E. P.

INTRODUCTION

THIS is a book of carols from the America we know as the United States, though their origins anticipated American independence by more than a hundred and fifty years. And it is perhaps fitting that their publication should coincide with the three-hundredth anniversary of the sailing of the *Mayflower*, without which folk song in America might have taken a different turn. This collection draws on both the mainstreams of American folk song, the Anglo-American and the Afro-American, but it is now possible to trace something of the growth of a third independent stream, American folk song proper, and to assess the end product. Although American folk song was not indigenous, it acquired its own personality in the course of a widespread process of assimilation and acculturation, many-factored, and often complex. Carols, as a part of folk song though not confined to it, are treated here not puristically, in accordance with the academic definition of the term ' carol ', but as covering the wide field of Christian Christmas song, carols as matured by tradition, in commonly accepted phraseology.

The earliest of America's imported collected song was European, the prescribed official religious song that travelled over with the Pilgrim Fathers as the hymnody of the Christian faith. Carols, the private home-made music of the folk, their unprescribed expression of the joyful celebration of a feast centred in the family, made the crossing unnoticed, undocumented. It is only today, towards the close of our century, that it has become possible to piece together something of the story of these small tenacious growths, to discover and rediscover the songs and their magic. This is largely due to the fine work of American scholars, now a literature of its own upon the subject; to the devoted enthusiasm of the American Folklore Society and the many field collectors over a vast area, who have watched, listened, recorded, and have sometimes been able to supply one isolated detail to add a vital link in the chain; and finally to the unrivalled Archive of Folk Song of the Library of Congress.

Although these two mainstreams of song in America had their genesis at about the same time – a few African slaves were landed in Virginia from Dutch ships in 1619, a year before the sailing of the *Mayflower* – the two folk cultures did not run concurrently. The lasting foundations of the Afro-American were laid in the eighteenth century, developing through the troubled years, to emerge with full impact only after the end of the Civil War. By 1727 there were 75,000 Negroes in the colonies of North America; by the 1790s more than 750,000; by 1800 over one million, more than 100,000 of them free. The twofold course of American folk song during this time and since, its co-existence and mutations, is a whodunnit experts have not finished debating. The debate lies outside the scope of this book, which exists primarily to make known the songs. But as pointers to what they are, whence they come, it may be helpful to chart a few landmarks.

When that fine scholar the Reverend Henry Ainsworth left the religious turmoil of Elizabethan England with the small band of Separatists from the Church who sought peace and freedom in the Low Countries from the religious persecutions of 1593, and found himself a lodging in a ' blind lane ' in Amsterdam, his decisive work was still to come. His *Psalter*, first printed in Amsterdam in 1612, was to found the Puritan settlers upon a rock – the *feste Burg* of the Lutheran hymnody that has persisted to this day. When succeeding generations in New England showed a preference for not foundering upon the rock but bypassing it to follow instead more wayward shoals of their own choosing, they declared an independence of their own and by force of circumstance took a new direction of consequence.

Ainsworth's *Psalter*, which sailed with the *Mayflower* Pilgrims in 1620, had a strong pedigree, its thirty-nine tunes taken mainly from *Sternhold and Hopkins*, 1562, with its continental infusion from the earlier *Genevan Psalter* of the English Protestant refugees in Switzerland – an instance of the valiant stronghold of song and its periodic stimulus by the pathetic human flights of history, to which we also owe the Psalms.

Though the Puritans viewed with suspicion any public music-making that could be regarded as frivolous, the settlers were zealous in the permitted use of sacred song. They depended on their voices. In the hazards of seventeenth-century navigation, linen chests took precedence over chests of viols. Among the settlers musical instruments are thought to have been few (see Percy Scholes, *The Puritans and Music*, Oxford, 1934). The majority of the Pilgrims were of country stock, unversed in the arts of the city, rural people who knew their folk tunes and their church tunes but did not look much beyond them. God-fearing, reared upon the foursquare granite of the Psalm paraphrases, they had in their earliest imported tune book all that sufficed them for their worship. Ainsworth's choice was sound. Orthodox in his belief in ' grave decent and comfortable singing ', he was emancipated enough to be flexible in his selection. As Waldo Selden Pratt has pointed out in *The Music of the Pilgrims* (Ditson, 1921), his *Psalter* is ' a document stemming from folk traditions, international in background, marked by a melodic freedom and rhythmic variety '.

It contained no carols. They travelled by word of mouth, the time-honoured language of tradition, in family intimacy, transplanted far from the Christmases whence they sprang. That first grim Christmas of the pilgrim company in the promised land was no joyful replica of the yule log festival of home. In ' New Plimouth' tree-felling began in earnest on 21 December, urgently needed to raise the first wattle-and-daub habitations of English traditional building. Work continued throughout Christmas Day 1620. (Except in its purely religious significance, the Puritans disapproved of Christmas.)

Armed with their faith and with Ainsworth's *Psalter*, they used the book as their staple song book for the next seventy years until after 1692, when they merged with the larger and more influential Massachusetts Bay Colony. *The Bay Psalm Book* printed in 1640 in Cambridge, Massachusetts, though it contained specific directions as to singing, had as yet no tunes. These followed for the first time in the enlarged Boston edition of 1698, its dominant influence that of English John Playford, with thirteen tunes together with his singing instructions from his *Introduction to the Skill of Music*, whose eleventh edition had appeared in London in 1687. In this tradition, the great names of Ravenscroft, Dowland, Tallis were held in respect by the educated settlers. The foundations of orthodox hymnody, the only organized communal singing the New Englanders knew, remained respectably conventional.

By the end of the eighteenth century it seems to have become as dreary and stereotyped as it became elsewhere. Life had gone out of it. The stock of tunes in use had dwindled to a handful. The practice of lining-out, by which the minister or elder read out the psalm line by line before the congregation sang it, a device common in England and Scotland and intended to help the illiterate, had its inevitable results. Sacred singing ground to a halt. The Anglican denominations were building organs and acquiring organists; the Puritans had neither. Hymns were often pitched high; the men sang the tune, the women screeched on top notes. Embellishments were popular, often disparate, in a vocal free-for-all. Contemporaneous accounts indicate that the cacophony must at times have been hair-raising.

Into this deadlock came a decisive change: the people opted for their own way of singing and their own songs, a trend set in motion once again by the currents of Christianity, this time from an unexpected quarter in a dramatic social-religious movement without parallel.

Camp meetings, or their equivalent, had erupted before. A train of mob enthusiasm had been sparked off by the preaching tours in England and

Ireland in 1799 and 1805 of the eloquent eccentric 'Crazy Dow', the American Methodist Lorenzo Dow, whose introduction of camp meetings in England in 1790 so rocked the camp as to lead to a split resulting in the severance of Primitive Methodists from Wesleyans.

In the New World the camp meetings of the Great Revival, whose spiritual driving force was the powerful oratory of the English preachers John Wesley and George Whitefield, were ably furthered by Jonathan Edwards of New England and the Presbyterian minister James McGready, whose missions during the years 1800–1805 blazed the trail for the Great Awakening in the trans-Allegheny West and the South. The camp meetings, which pushed frontierwards, sweeping west and south in the late 1700s and early 1800s, reached at their height an unprecedented scale. In the collaboration between Presbyterians, Baptists, and Methodists, the lead passed to Baptists and Methodists, the singing faiths that wooed the people with song and were to have a lasting influence on America's song. Bringing together in the cause of a common belief a pioneer people, often living in remote conditions, starved of the society of fellow-men beyond their own circle, lacking as yet the facilities of meeting houses, these huge gatherings were gregarious infectious outgoing festivals of eating out, singing out, sleeping out, communally worshipping out; mammoth religious singing picnics (and also matrimonial marts).

They occurred at a time when the oral sources of folk song were still relatively pure. Words were provided, to be fitted to a popular tune, both words and tune often so simple as to be little more than repetitive phrases, easy for anyone to pick up. Texts of Isaac Watts, Cennick, Wesley, Whitefield were pressed into service. The tunes people used for them were mainly the folk tunes they knew and sang by ear without thinking, a traditional process of adaptation whose workings have their parallels in the eleventh-century records of secular ballad tunes used for religious words, and in Luther, the Scottish Wedderburns, and Bach. And so we find Watts to a child's lullaby, 'The Sinner's Invitation' to 'The Braes o' Balquhidder', and 'Why do we mourn departing friends?' to 'When first I left old Ireland', and countless other matings and cross-fertilizations of words and tune.

It is fascinating to study the seed sown, its diverse and sometimes weird results in the wide and ready field; accident and circumstance alongside the zeal of planning and of racial mingling; Catholics active with plainsong – and, as Gilbert Chase recounts in his distinguished study, *America's Music* (McGraw-Hill, New York, 1955), the mission friars in California who were the proud possessors of an English barrel organ that played thirty tunes, among them a waltz, a hornpipe, a reel, and a tune called 'Go to the Devil'.

Although in the interchanges of the revivalist campaigns and the corresponding two-way exchange of songs it is sometimes difficult to make a case for definite origin on one side of the Atlantic or the other, common stock is identifiable, its modes and turn of phrase, their variations manifold: old tunes with added words; known words with borrowed tunes; collateral tunes; folk song relatives near or distant; families and types of song; crossbreed sports from venerable ballad stock; beautiful untraceable songs. In the best of those collected in America is a character and turn of phrase emergent as national, characteristically its own (see no. 24). And where but in an American setting of the Cherry Tree Carol (no. 14) could one find, in a picture of the Holy Family seen through Virginian eyes, the phrase ' And Joseph stood around '?

In the wake of the camp meetings came the early printed camp song books, the Sacred, Christian, Southern, Social *Harps, Harmonies, Repositories, Songsters*, the long-shaped fasola books so dear to the Baptists, printed in the fah-so-la 4-shape and 7-shape notation of the early American systems of solmization, treasuries from oral sources of secular folk song become sacred, in Pullen Jackson's phrase, folk song welded to the folk, the white spirituals which are a unique American contribution to world folk literature, and which in *The Sacred Harp* singing of Alabama have persisted as a living folk movement to this day.

The compilers of these song books were a tough and enterprising lot, mostly singing teachers of the singing schools that arose and multiplied with the people's desire to learn the notes and be taught ' regular ' singing. Most of them dedicated amateur musicians who acquired a remarkable degree of proficiency, they gave themselves to the task with commendable zeal. Jerry Ingalls, William Wyeth, Benjamin Franklin White and E. J. King, ' Singin' Billy' Walker, William Billings of the ' fuging' tunes, whose compositions are respected and sung today, are household names of these beautifully engraved collections of three-part writing (it is revealing that Walker, in his prefatory ' Dictionary of Musical Terms ', defines ' Air ' as ' the tenor part ').

There are few carols; those there are are in every respect worthy of representation (see nos. 1,2,3,6,27,29). The home-spun words, in varying degrees close to their traditional English forebears, have the familiar clichés, *mild/child, maid/laid*, and the inevitable *swaddling bands*; the familiarly modal tunes are splendidly vital and apt. From the wealth of folk tunes written down from this era and preserved, it is possible to gauge something of the extent of the carols which existed alongside in sung tradition, evidenced by the versions collected since, and which, for all their allegiance to older models, take on a new entity and individuality. In the

13

carols of English origin, it is remarkable to find a version of the Coventry Carol in Tennessee (no. 28), and in North Carolina the exquisite tune to 'Down in yon forest' (no. 10), variant of the Corpus Christi Carol of which, in its earliest and purest form, no traditional English tune has survived. Folk carols such as these surely deserve an established place in the whole English-speaking repertory.

It may be appropriate to remember that the term 'spiritual', shared by both white and coloured, implies its origin in the words of St Paul's exhortation to the early Christians as 'speaking one to another in psalms and hymns and spiritual songs, singing and making melody in your heart to the Lord' (Ephesians v.19), one preached by John Wesley, and taken literally by the New England settlers, who understood by it a type of song distinct from the psalms and hymns of conventional worship.

To Christmas the Negro brought the full glowing vitality of his own conception of it, characteristically visual, poetic, practical, closely related to his experience. At his hands the carol takes on a new liveliness in both words and tune, a tenderness and spontaneity as compelling as they are moving. Negro carols are characterized by a freedom and improvisatory flexibility which makes of them something wholly personal and individual, irresistible in their impetus and their relation to rhythm accompaniment. To these castaway people the home life of the family of Bethlehem was a reality close to their own. Who but they could have envisaged the little cradle as having got rhythm (no. 21), or the Gospel story with a railroad refrain (no. 15)?

With the bania (banjar), a West African instrument of the primitive form of hollowed-out gourd with skin drumhead and stretched strings, precursor of the banjo and the guitar, the Negroes brought instrumental accompaniment to their songs and a more communal tradition, as distinct from the unaccompanied solo type of Anglo-Saxon folk song – one of the most exciting importations in the history of music. They brought their way of singing and their forms of it: the graphic call-and-response, leader-and-group, question-and-answer of communal expression; and their inborn dance sense and rhythm, the beat in the blood, and the modified scale with its subtle ambiguities that were to become known as the' blue' notes of American jazz.

In plantation life, cut off from the relative sophistication of the city, the folk music of the slaves kept its language and developed in its own way at its own pace, work rather than piety its motivating force. Contact with white folk song and hymnody was gradual, its cumulative contact not strongly assimilated until the late eighteenth century, which brought evangelical Christianity to the southern plantations. Catholics, Episcopalians, Presbyterians, all were active. It was the breakaway denominations rather than the more orthodox creeds, the Methodists and Baptists with their particular appeal to the poor and oppressed, who had most to offer the enslaved. Their songs became an influence of acculturation and an undeniable element of the background of the Negro spiritual.

Much has been written of mutual influences, the interplay of white and black song. Miss Anne G. Gilchrist (1863–1954), active in the folk song revival in England, was an early pioneer ('The Folk Element in Early Revival Hymns and Tunes', *JFSS* viii, 83), and the authoritative comparative studies of the late Professor George Pullen Jackson, *Spiritual Folk-Songs of Early America* (Dover Publications, New York, 1937) and *Down-East Spirituals* (J. J. Augustin, New York, 1952), are the foundations of modern research in the subject. On it, the experts, as usual, do not agree: useful summaries are given by John W. Work in his preface to *American Negro Songs and Spirituals* (Bonanza Books, New York, 1940) and by Don Yoder, *Pennsylvania Spirituals* (Pennsylvania Folklife Society, 1961). Whatever the various contentions, it is scarcely possible not to admit certain common factors and their effects.

In a corpus of Negro song that has mostly remained remarkably pure, part of the difficulty in determining source details is caused by the lack of collection or documentation before 1840, as also of description of the songs' early stages and development. It was not until after the end of the Civil War in 1865 that Negro song was made known, from 1871 onwards by the Jubilee Singers of Fisk University and by other travelling singing groups from industrial schools and institutes founded for the advancement of Negro education, whose tours brought nationwide the revelation and impact of the Negro spiritual.

In this vast and complex canvas no more can be attempted here than an outline of focal points. All that remains may be filled in by anyone interested. The main thing is the songs themselves, here represented in their two main classes, with a smaller hybrid third of Anglo-American joint stock contribution (nos. 16, 23, 25, 37).

Because of the unfortunate difficulty in obtaining many of the books on the subject, a separate bibliography is not given, but it is hoped that the references contained in this introduction may serve as a useful lead towards further reading.

In the common meeting ground of the carol, from the dance song of primitive tribes to the round games of children, the Negro shares the basic stuff of his age-old expression with the rest of human kind. It is no paradox that in form and content, as also in spirit, some Negro songs of Christmas come near to the dance carol of early Christendom. In the fight for freedom, slave songs spoke in the sad symbolism of captivity. Beholding Bethlehem, black and white speak as one the language of wonder in the shining simplicity of the songs themselves, their living lovely value in the world today. The recurrent imagery of the Tree of Life has many forms. Mother Ann Lee, Shaker foundress and mystic, had a vision of America: ' I saw a large tree, every leaf of which shone with such brightness as made it appear like a torch '.

ELIZABETH POSTON

A NOTE ON PERFORMANCE

CONSIDERATION has been given to maximum flexibility and variety in the songs' treatment. Much can be done with the imaginative use of descant.

The guitar harmonies are suggested for single vocal line and do not relate to the piano accompaniments. The songs should be studied in type and character. For guitar accompaniment it is as pointless to add rhythm accompaniment totally out of character with the song, e.g. *Joseph and Mary* (*The Cherry Tree Carol*) (no. 14) or *I wonder as I wander* (no. 24), which require only the most spare and sensitively suggestive accompaniment, no more than a chord or stress here and there to underline tune and sense, as it is in keeping to accompany such rhythmical songs as *Come and I will sing you* (no. 12) or *Wasn't that a mighty day* (no. 42) with appropriate rhythm underlay. A guide as to type and treatment may usefully be taken from the piano accompaniments.

ABBREVIATIONS

AFS	Archive of Folk Song, Library of Congress, Washington, D.C.
Bramley and Stainer	Bramley and Stainer, *Christmas Carols*, 1867
Gilbert	Davies Gilbert, *Some Ancient Christmas Carols*, 1822
Hone	William Hone, *Ancient Mysteries Described*, 1823
Husk	W. H. Husk, *Songs of the Nativity*, 1868
JAFL	*Journal of American Folklore*, the American Folklore Society
JFSS	*Journal of the Folk Song Society* (1898), continued as *Journal of the English Folk Dance and Song Society* (after 1931)
Sandys	William Sandys, *Christmas Carols*, 1833
Sharp and Karpeles	Cecil Sharp, edited Maud Karpeles, *English Folk Songs from the Southern Appalachians*, 1932
Sylvester	'Joshua Sylvester' (pseudonym), *A Garland of Christmas Carols Ancient and Modern*, 1861
Tate and Brady	Nahum Tate and Nicholas Brady, *The New Version of Metrical Psalms*, 1696

NOTES ON THE CAROLS

1 A VIRGIN MOST PURE (A Virgin unspotted). The tune and first verse of the words are in Wyeth's *Repository of Sacred Music Part Second* of John Wyeth, Harrisburg, Pa., 1820 (reprinted by the Da Capo Press, New York, 1964), where it is called 'Christmas Hymn' and is printed in shape-notes in three parts, the melody in the middle part. This tune-book is an important collection of sacred folk songs or white spirituals compiled and published to meet the needs of the camp meetings of Pennsylvania of the period.

The American version of the carol is close to the English folk carol, which was widespread and had various tunes. Cecil Sharp gives four versions (*JFSS* v, 24ff.). The carol's popularity in England is attested by three variants of the words in Cecil Sharp's Book of Broadsides as well as by its appearance in *Gilbert, Sandys, Husk* and other nineteenth-century collections. The eminent American authority, Professor George Pullen Jackson, in *Down-East Spirituals and Others* (J. J. Augustin, New York, 2nd edition, 1953), gives verses 1–5 with the tune and quotes the carol as having been found in a 4-shape-note manuscript song book made in Maryland between 1800 and 1830. It appears even earlier in J. Arnold's *Compleat Psalmodist* of 1750. The opinion of Vaughan Williams that the tune travelled from England across the Channel is borne out by its appearance more recently in a folk song collection from Bavaria in which it has the title 'The English Greeting'. Verse 5 is as in *Husk*, with its traditional imagery, beloved of Renaissance painters, of the celestial choir standing in the sky, as might be the muster of any organized choral society. John Wyeth (1770–1858) was a Unitarian publisher and bookseller, editor of a Harrisburg weekly newspaper.

2 BABE OF BETHLEHEM (Ye nations all, on you I call). This jolly, bustling tune, probably of folk origin, occurs only in *The Southern Harmony*, 4-shape-note song book compiled at Spartanburg, South Carolina, and printed at New Haven, Connecticut, 1835 (reprint: Pennsylvania 1854 edition by Hastings House, New York, 1939) by William ('Singin' Billy') Walker, who added to it a treble and a bass part. The text with another good tune is also in *The Sacred Melodeon*, compiled by A. S. Hayden (Cincinnati, *c.* 1848). Dr Frank C. Brown, in his *Collection of North Carolina Folklore* (Duke University Press, Durham, N.C., 1952), iii, 554, records an amusing oral corruption of the words of verse 1, line 2, as 'Come view this sacred ration'. He received line 5 as 'loyal Jews'. The graceful phraseology of the text (e.g. verse 5 line 7) points to eighteenth-century usage.

William Walker (1808–75) of Spartanburg, South Carolina, leading singing master, compiler of folk tunes to sacred words, was of Welsh descent and a Baptist. He taught music for forty-five years and his collection was a handbook used in his singing schools throughout the south-eastern states.

3 COME AWAY TO THE SKIES. From *The Southern Harmony*, compiled by William Walker (1808–75) (reprint: Pennsylvania 1854 edition by Hastings House, New York, 1939; see Note 2). The vigorous tune 'Exultation' has folk song affinities and an ending describable as of common folk song stock (cf. 'Come all you Virginia girls', *The Penguin Book of American Folk Songs*, Lomax and Poston, p. 40). Probably an American tune of earlier date, it was collected also in Alabama from family tradition. The words are a slightly altered version of a poem by Charles Wesley (1707–88), first published in his *Hymns for Families*, 1767 (165), subsequently in 1780 in the *Wesleyan Hymn Book* (478). They were retained in further editions of that collection and are in other Methodist and some American hymnals. In their original form Wesley wrote them on 12 October 1755, his wife's anniversary, under the title of 'On the twenty-ninth birthday of a Friend'.

4 WATTS'S CRADLE SONG. The words are associated with a version of the tune 'Restoration' in *The Southern Harmony* (see Note 2). The poems of Isaac Watts (1674–1748), Nonconformist hymn-writer, a native of Southampton, were an English importation of the Wesleyan American missions and much favoured in Revivalist song.

5 The second tune is that of a favourite children's folk lullaby rhyme, sung nationwide variously as ' Go tell Aunt Nancy/Aunt Rhody/Aunt Tabbie etc.' (see *The Penguin Book of American Folk Songs*, Lomax and Poston, p. 58). Jean-Jacques Rousseau used a similar melody for an air in his opera *Le Devin du Village* (1752), a simple tune of basic traditional currency, probably the forebear of the still popular American tune.

6 SHEPHERDS, REJOICE. Words and tune from *The Social Harp*, fasola song book compiled by the Baptist John Gordon McCurry, Andersonville, Georgia, printed in Philadelphia in 1855. Also in *The Sacred Harp* of B. F. White and E. J. King (Philadelphia, 1844), a classic collection of Old Baptist revival spirituals with traditional tunes of British origin (facsimile reprint 1859 edition: Broadman Press, Nashville, Tennessee, 1968). The song was known earlier; the words appear in *A Collection of Spiritual Songs used at the Camp Meetings and in the Great Revival in the United States of America*, printed in Newry, Northern Ireland, 1817. They paraphrase those of Nahum Tate (1652–1715), 'While shepherds watched their flocks by night' in *Tate and Brady* (1696). Cited in another version and variant of tune and words (*Knoxville Harmony*, 1838; and *The Social Harp*, 1855) in *Another Sheaf of White Spirituals* by G. Pullen Jackson (University of Florida Press).

7 AWAY IN A MANGER. The words first appeared in print in *A Little Children's Book for Schools and Families*, published in 1885 by the Evangelical Lutheran Church in North America. The tune was written for them by William James Kirkpatrick (1838–1921), American composer and director of church music.

8 The second tune, a Basque traditional melody, attaches to the words as an alternative favourite in England.

9 RISE UP, SHEPHERD, AN' FOLLER. Christmas Plantation Song, printed in *Religious Folk Songs of the Negro as sung on the Plantations*, edited by Thomas P. Fenner, Virginia, 1909. One of the many Negro spirituals collected during the Civil War, mainly from Negroes of the islands off the coasts of Georgia and South Carolina and published in 1867 as *Slave Songs of the United States*, compiled by William Francis Allen, Charles Pickard Ware, and Lucy McKim Garrison in 1867 (reprint: Oak Publications, New York, 1965). Related tunes are found in English and Welsh folk song; a similar tune was sung in the Isle of Man and in Wales as a carol (*Journal of Welsh Folksong* ii, 182 ff.); and a form of the melody appears in an early American hymn 'He was found worthy' (*Songs of Grace*, Lorenz and Baltzell).

10 DOWN IN YON FOREST. This striking version collected by John Jacob Niles in North Carolina is closely related to its counterparts, the English folk versions of the sixteenth-century text known as the Corpus Christi Carol (Balliol College, Oxford. MS. 354):

> Lully, lulley, lully, lulley,
> The faucon hath borne my make away

the mystical Eucharistic carol in the language and imagery of chivalry. The Scottish traditional version 'The heron flew east, the heron flew west' is close to the English text. An English folk version from North Staffordshire is quoted by Sir Frank Sidgwick in *Notes and Queries* (1862); one from Derbyshire was published by Vaughan Williams. Peter Warlock (1894–1930) used the Balliol text in his modern setting.

The Derbyshire version has a direct reference to Christmas in the last verse only, one which seems to have been tacked on as ending on a more cheerful note after the preceding austere and sombre verses, a switch of mood paralleled in the last verse of the North Carolina version. The reference to the blossoming thorn in verse 5 Derbyshire and to the shrub tree in verse 5 North Carolina derives from the legend of the Holy Thorn of Glastonbury.

11 THE BLESSINGS OF MARY. Words and tune collected by Richard Chase from the singing of Mr Will Brady, Carthage, North Carolina, who said: 'That's a precious song, somebody ought to take care of it' (*JAFL* vol. 48, no. 390, 1935). The English carol 'The Joys of Mary' appears first in its fifteenth century form in Brit. Mus. MS. Sloane 2593, in which the joys are five. In later versions they grow: in *Bramley and Stainer* they are seven; *Sandys* gives twelve. American versions of the words from Pennsylvania and Connecticut are in *JAFL* v, 1892; from West Virginia in *Folk Songs of the South* by David Harrington Cox (Harvard University Press, 1925); John Jacob Niles collected words and tune in the Southern Appalachian Mountains; and a version of both was found in Massachusetts.

12 COME AND I WILL SING YOU, a form of the 'Carol of the Twelve Numbers', belongs to a class of cumulative song of several names, e.g. 'Green grow the

rashes, O', 'The Dilly Song', and of considerable antiquity, its earliest form traceable to the Hebrew version in the Service for the First Night of the Passover. The song occurs in various forms in England, from thence in America. In Sharp, *Folk Songs from Somerset*, 1911, 'The Dilly Song'; in Lucy Broadwood and J. A. Fuller Maitland, *English County Songs*, 1893, 'The Twelve Apostles'; and *Sharp and Karpeles* give six variants (*JFSS* i, 90–94). See also *JAFL* xxx, 335–6. Most of the versions have common denominators; all agree in the symbolism of One, the God 'whose name shall be One' (Zechariah xiv.9). The song's fascination lies largely in its incantatory magic and the weird and garbled lines, some nonsensical, that have crept in down the centuries, all, whether sense or nonsense, the long accretions of a folk ritual of striking effect.

The two versions given here, nos. 12 and 13, both have a basis in the original biblical significance, the present version with an infectious infusion of nonsense. It was given to the late John Goss on a ranch in Washington State by a roving character known as Skillum who sang it at many a camp fire. The two Chrissymas babes conform to the accepted reference as to the infant Christ and St John Baptist. The significance of green is uncertain but would seem to carry implications of the ancient lore of the greenwood. The three in Bethlea refers presumably to the Holy Family in Bethlehem, the word sometimes thus abbreviated in American folk singing. Six, according to some versions, including the French Canadian, refers to the six waterpots of the miracle of Cana of Galilee (John II.309), though it makes scant sense here. The more obvious interpretation of the seven shiners is the constellation of the Plough (*Ursa Major*); the mystical interpretation is that of the seven stars in the right hand of the Son of Man in the vision of St John the Divine (Revelation I.10–16). Eight is corrupt (? fellowship white – possibly the blessed souls of the heavenly host). Nine is perhaps a local allusion to promontories of the Pacific seaboard all named by the early navigators after the same woman. Eleven is generally accepted as referring to the Apostles without Judas; twelve, as the twelve Apostles. The song is a splendid one for group singing, particularly with guitar, and goes hurling forward with unbroken impetus from start to finish.

13 CHILDREN, GO WHERE I SEND THEE! The Negro version of the 'Carol of the Twelve Numbers', also in group form, sticks fairly closely to formula. Three is ascribable to Shadrach, Meshach, and Abednego of the Burning Fiery Furnace (Daniel III). The Hebrew version has the patriarchs Abraham, Isaac, and Jacob. Some English and Appalachian versions attach three to the corruption 'wisers' for the three Wise Men from the East (Matthew II.1–2). Four is generally accepted as referring to the Four Evangelists. Five, six, and seven are debatable – seven is also rhymed as 'went to heav'n'. Eight has been attached to Noah's family of eight in the Ark: Noah and his wife and his three sons, each son with his wife (Genesis VI.10; VII.7). Nine is thought to refer to the nine orders or choirs of Angels (Revelation V.11), traditionally depicted as beings in shining garments and usefully enumerated in the words of Athelstan Riley's hymn:

> Ye watchers and ye holy ones,
> Bright Seraphs, Cherubim and Thrones,
>   Raise the glad strain, Alleluia!
> Cry out, Dominions, Princedoms, Powers,
> Virtues, Archangels, Angels, choirs. . . .

This version has a characteristic declaimed question line and then swings along in rhythm to its syncopated refrain.

14 JOSEPH AND MARY (The Cherry Tree Carol) – really a ballad and widely current in European folklore, bearing traces of its early antecedents in the legend from the apocryphal gospel of pseudo-Matthew in which the tree, true to local colour, is a date-palm. In European versions it becomes apple and cherry. The cherry tree version is in the Coventry play of *The Miraculous Birth and the Midwives*; also in English broadsides; and in *Hone, Sandys, Sylvester* and *Husk*. Sharp and Karpeles collected it in the Southern Appalachians (*Folk Songs from the Southern Appalachians*, Oxford, 1932, i, 90 ff., six variants); John Jacob Niles in Kentucky (*Seven Mountain Songs*, 1928, G. Schirmer Inc., New York). Also *JAFL* xlv, 13; xxix, 293 and 417; *JFSS* iii, 260. This exquisitely meditative tune from Kentucky (*AFS* 1010 A[1]) is a solo-type folk ballad of outstanding beauty, the simple parable a quaint and touching instance of the domestic scene as envisaged through the eyes of simple folk and applied to the Holy Family.

The allusion in stanza 9 to Christ's birthday is in keeping with the song's antiquity. 25 December was appointed by the Roman emperor Aurelian in A.D. 274 as the festival in Rome of the unconquered sun (*natalis solis invicti*), celebrations of the winter solstice that were transformed by the Christian church into the festivals of Christmas and Epiphany in which various pre-Christian elements survived. The date of Christ's birth, near to the Feast of the Passover, is unknown. The first mention of the Feast of the Nativity as being on 25 December occurs in a Roman almanac for Christians of A.D. 354, although Christmas had been celebrated on that date in Rome since at least eighteen years earlier. In the eastern part of the Roman empire the birth and the baptism of Jesus were celebrated on 6 January, the day on which Christmas is still observed by the Armenian Church. In the course of the fourth century the celebration of Christmas on 25 December was adopted in the east except by Jerusalem. In the west its observance on that date spread from Rome to become general in the sixth century, the two great Christian festivals of winter remaining closely linked in the Twelve Days of Christmas.

15 MARY HAD A BABY. St Helena Spiritual, the tune and stanza 1 collected by N. G. J. Ballanta-Taylor in *St Helena Island Spirituals* (Penn Community Services Inc., Frogmore, S.C., 1925), the remaining verses as sung variously extempore. See also *The Book of American Negro Spirituals*; *The Second Book of Negro Spirituals* by James Weldon Johnson and J. Rosamond Johnson (The Viking Press, New York, 1925). A happy example of simple story-telling in question-and-answer. The imaginative impact upon the mind of the Negro of the advent of the railroad, 1830–40, is reflected in the sort of refrain in true ballad

tradition, in which there is nothing incongruous in a refrain not necessarily related to the matter of the song. A true community song, this spiritual lends itself adaptively to individual treatment: solo/smaller group question-and-answer within the group, its gentle rhythmical insistence effective with many voices or few.

16 THE THREE KINGS OF ORIENT (Epiphany Carol), written and composed (*c.* 1857) by Dr John Henry Hopkins jr. (1820–91), Rector of Christ's Church, Williamsport, son of J. H. Hopkins, Bishop of Vermont, and writer of hymns and carols. In its skilful exploitation of the story, and the opportunities it affords for treatment in character, the setting has endeared itself on both sides of the Atlantic. It is adapted here for three voices unaccompanied and with optional instrumental descant; and is given also in the composer's harmonization.

17 GO TELL IT ON THE MOUNTAIN from *Religious Songs of the Negro as sung on the Plantations*, edited by Thomas P. Fenner, 1909. A song impressive in its dignity and faith, the tune reminiscent of the 'Battle Hymn of the Republic'. The rhythm of the refrain should be kept very steady.

18, 19 CHARLES IVES'S CAROL (Little Star of Bethlehem). Charles Edward Ives (1874–1954), son of a military bandmaster in Danbury, Connecticut, musician and businessman, composed after his daily work in an insurance office and wrote most of his most important music between 1906 and 1916, though recognition did not come until some thirty years later, towards the end of his life. Some of his best music is intimately related to the American scene, and he is recognized today as an original mind whose experimentation was in advance of his time, anticipating developments to come in twentieth-century music. This little carol, written before 1900, has a characteristically individual last line. Its gentle syncopations are highly effective and should not be dragged, since to lose their rhythm is to lose their piquancy.

20 LONGFELLOW'S CAROL (I Heard the Bells on Christmas Day), its sentiments still appropriate, is here fitted to the beautiful tune of folk derivation, 'Perseverance', slightly adapted from Wyeth's *Sacred Repository Part Second*, 1820 (reprinted by the Da Capo Press, New York, 1964). See also Note 1.

21 CHILD OF GOD (The little cradle rocks tonight in glory). The tune and first stanza were collected by R. Emmett Kennedy and published in *Mellows* (A. & C. Boni Inc., New York, 1925). 'Mellows' to the Negroes of southern Louisiana were melodies, in particular those of their devotional song. The remaining stanzas of this enchantingly imaginative evocation of Christmas were collected independently by Emma M. Backus in 'Christmas Carols in Georgia' (*JAFL* xii, 272, 1899). The tune is nearly related to that of a children's singing game (see Elizabeth Poston, *The Children's Song Book*, The Bodley Head, London, 1961; Dufour Editions, U.S.A.).

22 POOR LI'L JESUS, also from *Mellows* (see Note 21), a Louisiana version of a moving Negro carol collected from the singing of a coloured Baptist preacher. Another instance of refrain dissociated from stanza, in this case at variance with the sense of the final verse (see also Note 15). In *The Cambridge Hymnal* (Cambridge University Press, 1967), the first modern hymn book to include this carol, there printed with another tune, the final refrain line is modified, for convenience' sake in the sense, to 'No more a pity an' a shame'. The song's slow pulse and strong melody make it particularly effective with guitar or other plucked or keyboard instrument.

23 JESUS CHRIST THE APPLE TREE. Suitable for all times and seasons, this song is not specifically a Christmas song. It is included here because of its association with Christmas in the carol services and broadcasts of the choir of King's College, Cambridge, who have also recorded it (EMI ALP/ASD 2290). The beautiful visionary words in the imagery of the Tree of Life are printed without tune in Joshua Smith's *Divine Hymns or Spiritual Songs*, Portsmouth, New Hampshire, 1784.

24 I WONDER AS I WANDER, collected by John Jacob Niles in North Carolina (*Songs of the Hill-Folk*, G. Schirmer Inc., New York, Set 14 of Schirmer's American Folk Song Series), a meditative solo-type folk song that should sound essentially free and improvisatory with only the lightest suggestion of accompaniment to the reflective vocal line.

25 O LITTLE TOWN OF BETHLEHEM (Forest Green). Included in *The Penguin Book of Christmas Carols* (with the harmonization of the late R. Vaughan Williams) and printed also here because, with its shared claim on either side of the Atlantic and the general affection in which it is held, it could scarcely be omitted. The English traditional tune 'The Ploughboy's Dream', renamed by Vaughan Williams 'Forest Green', and the American words of Phillips Brooks (1835–93), Bishop of Massachusetts, a renowned preacher and a good man, are together an Anglo-American Christmas classic.

26 JUDA'S LAND. Appalachian carol of unknown record in the folk song collection of the Hutchins Library, Berea College, Kentucky, used here by kind permission. As the text of this attractive carol is short, it is suggested that the carol be sung to terminate with a reprise of stanza 1 and chorus.

27 JESUS BORN IN BETHLEHEM. From the Frank C. Brown *Collection of North Carolina Folklore* (Duke University Press, Durham, N.C., 1952, no. 537: iii, 595; and v, 337), one of a number of versions of similar words and tune. In early editions of *The Sacred Harp* (1859, with one stanza); with fuller text in *The Christian Songster* of Joseph Bever, Dayton, Ohio, 1858. Also in Annabel Morris Buchanan, *Folk Hymns of America* (J. & J. Fischer, New York, 1938), southern version; collected by John Jacob Niles in Virginia; by *Sharp and Karpeles* (ii, 210) in North Carolina.

28 LULLE LULLAY, collected by John Jacob Niles (*Ten Christmas Carols from the Appalachian Mountains*, G. Schirmer Inc., New York, Set 16 of Schirmer's American Folk Song Series). A striking instance of the transplant to Tennessee of the Coventry Carol (see *The Penguin Book of Christmas Carols*, pp. 24, 64–5). Except for the corruption in stanza 1 ('persevere' instead of 'preserve') and the addition of a regrettable last verse, the American folk version of the text is pretty faithful to its English sixteenth-century counterpart of the *Pageant of Shearmen and Tailors*. In this play the carol is designated in a note by a later hand as a song 'the women sing'. As such, it was an exception, as women did not take part in the drama of the day, either religious or secular, except in such a special instance where dramatic propriety and faithfulness to the biblical story allowed the participation of female religious. The addition in the American version of the sentimental stanza 5 is given here for the sake of completeness, though this verse may well be omitted in performance. The shapely and singable folk tune differs totally from the traditional English ¾ setting in parts, and is essentially of solo/unison type.

29 SHEPHERDS IN JUDEA (As shepherds in Jewry), a version of freshness and charm, with the emphasis on the shepherds, of the English traditional Davies Gilbert carol 'A Virgin most pure' (see no. 1, p. 34). According to George Pullen Jackson this carol is to be found only in *The Christian Harmony or Songster's Companion* compiled by Jeremiah Ingalls in Exeter, New Hartford, 1805.

The early musicians of New England were a tough breed ready to turn their hand to anything. Jeremiah Ingalls (1764–1828), singing-school teacher, composer and compiler of music, sometime farmer and cooper, was a native of Massachusetts. He built himself a house in Vermont which he kept as a tavern and was a deacon of the Congregational Church, where he led the choir. He had a number of children and directed his family band on the bass viol. He was folk-song-minded and of lively humour – many of his tunes derive from secular songs and dances, and he liked them gay.

30 HEAV'N BELL-A RING, South Carolina, from *Slave Songs of the United States*, 1867 (reprint: Oak Publications, New York, 1965 – see Note 9). From a longer text, the Christmas verses are expressive of the Negro's response in elation and excitement to the summons of the chapel bell to worship and song.

31 WHAT YOU GONNA CALL YO' PRETTY LITTLE BABY? Traditional Negro Christmas spiritual (general), of characteristic simplicity in question-and-answer form and strong rhythm. An earlier version is 'Mary, what yer gwine er name dat Purty Leetle Baby' in *Southern Thoughts for Northern Thinkers* by Jeannette Robinson Murphy (Bandanna Publishing Co., New York, 1904).

32 OH, MARY AND THE BABY, SWEET LAMB, Texas. *AFS* 913 B². A song of simple repetitive formula combining characteristically the moving, the tender, and the gay.

33 LAST MONTH O' THE YEAR (When was Jesus born?). Christmas watch-night spiritual, one of a number of versions in group-and-response form. (See also, with another tune, *The Penguin Book of American Folk Songs*, Lomax and Poston, p. 84.)

34 O MARY, WHERE IS YOUR BABY? Louisiana, in *Mellows*, R. Emmett Kennedy (A. & C. Boni Inc., New York, 1925 – see Note 21). A spiritual of the Holy Innocents, an unusual subject in Negro songs of this type. The tempo of the verse should be treated with some freedom; the refrain moves in strict rhythm.

35 VIRGIN MARY, MEEK AND MILD, Kentucky, collected John Jacob Niles (*Seven Negro Exaltations*, G. Schirmer Inc., New York). This curious and amusing song is part of a longer one called ' Trip to Raleigh ', of which the first four stanzas are rumbustious ballad joggerel nothing to do with Christmas, but, according to John Jacob Niles, a work song recorded also as ' Shoot dat Buffey '. He collected it in this form from the singing of a Negro bootblack in Kentucky in 1912, and later found it with longer text in Tennessee. The refrain still has nothing to do with Christmas. These three ebullient verses in which the song suddenly changes direction and becomes a spiritual are, as Mr Niles rightly points out, the interesting ones, and they go roaring ahead, infectious in their high spirits.

36 SUNNY BANK (Christmas Day in the morning). This Virginia version in the *University of Virginia* (manuscript) *Collection of Folk-Music* (no. 183) was collected by Winston Wilkinson in Charlottesville, Virginia, in 1936 from the singing of Arthur Morris, and is cited in *Down-East Spirituals* by George Pullen Jackson (J. J. Augustin, New York, 2nd edition, 1953), pp. 63–4. In tune identical with the English children's rhyme and singing game ' Here we go round the mulberry bush ', in words an amalgam of English text variants, with a slight difference in the last line (see *The Penguin Book of Christmas Carols*, no. 8, pp. 48–9 and 22–3), the carol, with its artless gay simplicity, is an obvious importation. Its earliest version is in Forbes's *Cantus* (Aberdeen, 1666). An American version is in Marcus Lafayette Swan's *The New Harp of Columbia*, 1867, where it is incongruously attached to words by Charles Wesley (1707–88), ' O glorious hope of perfect love '. In England it has been found in many parts of the country, and the words are printed in *Husk* and broadsides.

The reference to the three ships is thought to derive from the legend of Les Saintes-Maries-de-la-Mer of the Camargue in Provence, which tells how St Mary, sister of the Virgin, and Mary, the mother of the Apostles James and John, together with St Mary Magdalene and Sarah, their Ethiopian servant, fled there from persecution in the Holy Land across the water. To Les Saintes-Maries the gipsies make spring pilgrimage each May to honour the shrine of their ancestress Sarah.

37 IT CAME UPON THE MIDNIGHT CLEAR (Noel). A favourite hybrid on either side. The traditional tune in Sir Arthur Sullivan's arrangement is related to Eardisley (*English Hymnal*, 601), an English folk tune collected in Herefordshire

in 1905. The words, by the Rev. Edmund Hamilton Sears (1810–76), Unitarian minister in Massachusetts and hymn writer (*Sermons and Songs of the Christian Life*, 1875), were first published in the magazine *The Christian Register*, 1850. Line 4 of stanza 5 has been slightly amended in accordance with modern practice inimical to the 'age of gold', so avoiding a reference inappropriate to our time without damage to the moving sincerity of the hymn as a whole.

38 SISTER MARY HAD-A BUT ONE CHILD. Christmas spiritual from the southeastern states, its refrain a heartrending Negro expression of direct experience.

39 SWEEP, SWEEP AND CLEANSE YOUR FLOOR. Shaker ritual song from *New Lebanon Hymnal*, attributed to Eleanor Potter, 1839.

The Mother referred to was Mother Ann Lee (1736–84), the remarkable Manchester woman of poor labouring stock, who became mystic and leader and broke away from an oppressed unhappy life and founded in 1774 the American sect of primitive Christianity known as the Shakers (from the bodily shaking of its members under the influence of spiritual exaltation). Originating in Bolton and Manchester during a Quaker revival in England in 1747, the Shaker movement, radical and pacifist, had lofty and austere ideals of life and works. Shakers believed in the second coming of Christ, and though they did not enforce celibacy, they practised it – a natural enough reaction to the squalor of the workers' lives and the grim tribulations of women. The emigrant Shakers settled in Watervliet near Albany, N.Y. A colony of converts was added near New Lebanon, and by the end of the century their numbers had increased, to swell at the movement's height to about six thousand in the second quarter of the nineteenth century, though after the Civil War the movement declined and in the present century dwindled to a few.

In what was certainly one of the most interesting of religious concepts, its members expressed the love and worship of God in physical movement and song, a mystical synthesis of powers which they practised with simple and fervent dedication. They encouraged the creativity of song and wrote down their tunes as best they could, in the manner in which they were sung, as folk song. These tunes did not conform to the standard type of hymn tune, but were spontaneous, unsophisticated, and often made use of current dance forms of the day (the present one a form of polka, cf. the English rhyme 'Tom, Tom, the piper's son'). Shaker songs and dances were a folk art, communal and decorous, men and women taking part together, each keeping their respective ranks. The Shakers applied the principle of ritual dance also to acts of daily life, as at Christmas time, in the age-old tradition of sweeping and garnishing the house in honour of Christ's birth. The historian of the Shakers, Edward D. Andrews, in his fascinating study *The Gift to be Simple* (Dover Publications, New York, 1940), has collected together a number of Shaker songs from which this one is taken.

40 SAINT STEPHEN AND HEROD, Vermont. A ballad with an interesting pedigree, collected in 1934 by Helen Hartness Flanders (*Ballads Migrant in New England*

by Helen Hartness Flanders and Marguerite Olney, Farrar, Straus & Young, New York, 1953) from Mr George L. Edwards of Vermont, a native of Northumberland, who remembered it from the singing of his grandmother of Seaton in the East Riding of Yorkshire.

Professor Bronson notes that the text is close to the fifteenth-century text in Brit. Mus. Sloane MS. 2593, *fol*. 22*b*. In F. E. Child, *The English and Scottish Popular Ballads*, Boston, 1882–98, no. 22; Bertrand Harris Bronson, *The Traditional Tunes of the Child Ballads* (Princeton University Press, 1959), i, 297.

The boar's head with gastronomic details of its serving features in other early English Christmas carols as a dish of festive importance (see R. L. Greene, *The Early English Carols*, Oxford, 1935).

41 BABY BORN TODAY (Mother Mary, what is the matter?), Georgia. A traditional watch-night 'shout'. The shout was a spontaneous improvisational form of song often accompanied by clapping and a shuffle-step known as shouting, traditionally sung by the Negroes at Baptist Christmas Eve watch-night service. The tune was sung to John Goss in New York State about 1939 by Ella Garrett, a southern singer who gave only two verses. The text here is from Robert W. Gordon, *Folk-Songs of America* (The New York Times Company, 1927–8).

42 WASN'T THAT A MIGHTY DAY, South Carolina and Tennessee. Traditional tune in N. G. J. Ballanta-Taylor, *St Helena Island Spirituals* (Penn Community Services Inc., Frogmore, S.C., 1925). Words in 'Some Negro Folk Songs from Tennessee' by Anna Kranz Odum (*JAFL* xxvii, 264, 1924). These words have an amusing corruption: 'David' for 'Jesus' in line 1 of stanza 2, and in the last line 'The beefsteak keep-a him warm', wording noted and corrected by Ballanta-Taylor. John W. Work in *American Negro Songs and Spirituals* (Bonanza Books, Crown Publishers Inc., New York, 1940) gives another stanza and a different tune.

43 THE TWELVE DAYS OF CHRISTMAS, Florida. *AFS* 989 A^1. The twelve days of Christmas (see Note 14), linking Christmas on 25 December and the Feast of the Epiphany on 6 January, were pronounced a festal tide by the Council of Tours in 567. This ancient cumulative song and forfeit game, common to England and France, America and French Canada, dates back to a thirteenth-century manuscript in the Library of Trinity College, Cambridge (B. 14. 39) entitled 'Twelfth Day'. The text reappears in *Mirth without Mischief*, a children's book published in London about 1780. There are a number of versions American and British: *JAFL* 13, 230; 18, 57; 30, 365; 46, 46; *JFSS* v, 277; *FLJ* vii, 244; Alice Bertha (Lady) Gomme, *The Traditional Games of England, Scotland, and Ireland*, 1894–8 (reprint: Dover Publications, New York, 1964), four versions. See also *JAFL* xxx, 365–6.

The tune of the American version given here is as good as the version currently used in England, popularly believed to be a traditional tune, but spurious to the extent that a salient phrase was written in, 'concertized' and copyrighted. The words are energetically rural. All versions generally agree as to the last six lines, which constitute a refrain. Of those collected in America the other lines have metaphors which contrast significantly with the tamer imagery of the British Isles – eleven bears a-leapin' (Vermont); nine wolves a-howling, eight deers a-running (Missouri), etc. In American or English, four colley/colored birds is acceptable; ' part of a juniper tree ' (as in *JAFL* 18, 57) for ' partridge in a pear tree ' is suspect, for the French equivalent (Franche-Comté) has the real partridge (*perdriole*), a word not susceptible of distortion and so confirming the sense.

THE CAROLS

A VIRGIN MOST PURE

Wyeth's Repository of Sacred Music, *1820, arr. E. P.*

death, hell and sin, Which A - dam's trans -

A D C A

- gress - ion in - volv - ed us — in.

D G C G

REFRAIN

poco f

Then let us be mer - ry, cast sor - rows a - way; Our

poco f

C D G A D

give a little _ _ _ _ _ _

Sav - ior, Christ   Je - sus,   was   born   on   this   day.

dim.

C   A   D   G   C   G

1 A virgin most pure, as the prophets foretold,
   Should bring forth a Savior which now we behold,
   To be our redeemer from death, hell and sin,
   Which Adam's transgression involvèd us in.
     Then let us be merry, cast sorrows away;
     Our Savior, Christ Jesus, was born on this day.

2 Through Bethlehem city in Jewry it was
   That Joseph and Mary together did pass;
   And for to be taxèd when thither they came,
   Since Caesar Augustus commanded the same.

3 But Mary's full time being come, as we find,
   That brought forth her first born to serve all mankind;
   The inn being full, for this heavenly guest,
   No place there was found for to lay him to rest.

4 But Mary, blest Mary, so meek and so mild,
   Soon wrappèd in swaddlings this heavenly child;
   Contented she laid him where oxen did feed,
   The great God of nature approved of the deed.

5 Then presently after, the shepherds did spy
   Vast numbers of angels to stand in the sky;
   So merrily talking, so sweet did they sing:
   All glory and praise to our heavenly King.

Verse 1: Wyeth's Repository of **Sacred Music Part** Second, *1820.*
Verses 2–5: shape-note song book 1800–1830

2

BABE OF BETHLEHEM

The Southern Harmony, *1854, arr. E. P.*

*omitting D♯

glo - rious news Of Je - sus and _ sal - va - tion. To

"roy - al _ Jews came first the _ news Of Christ the great Mes -

- si - ah," As was fore - told _ by pro - phets old, I -

Em   B7*   Em   B7*   Em

B7*   Em   B7*   Em   B7*

Em   B7*   Em   B7*   Em   B7*

- sa - iah, Je - re - mi - ah.

Em   B7*   Em   B7*   Em   B7*
                                     Fine Em

1 Ye nations all, on you I call,
  Come hear this declaration,
  And don't refuse this glorious news
  Of Jesus and salvation.
  To royal Jews came first the news
  Of Christ the great Messiah,
  As was foretold by prophets old,
  Isaiah, Jeremiah.

2 To Abraham the promise came,
  And to his sons forever,
  A light to shine in Isaac's line,
  By Scripture we discover.
  Hail! promised morn, the Savior's
    born,
  The glorious mediator,
  God's blessed Word made flesh and
    blood
  Assumed the human nature.

3 His parents poor in earthly store
  To entertain the stranger,
  They found no bed to lay his head,
  But in the ox's manger;
  No royal things, as used by kings,
  Were seen by those around him,
  But in the hay the stranger lay
  With swaddling bands around him.

4 On the same night a glorious light
  To shepherds there appearèd;
  Bright angels came in shining flame,
  They saw and greatly fearèd;
  The angels said, 'Be not afraid,
  Although we much alarm you,
  We do appear good news to bear,
  As now we will inform you.

5 'The city's name is Bethlehem,
  In which God hath appointed
  This glorious morn a Savior's born
  For him God hath anointed.
  By this you'll know, if you will go
  To see this little stranger,
  His lovely charms in Mary's arms,
  Both lying in a manger.'

6 When this was said, straightway
    was made
  A glorious sound from heaven;
  Each flaming tongue an anthem
    sung,
  'To men a Savior's given.
  In Jesus' name, the glorious theme,
  We elevate our voices,
  At Jesus' birth be peace on earth,
  Meanwhile all heaven rejoices.'

7 Then with delight they took their flight,
   And wing'd their way to glory;
   The shepherds gazed and were amazed
   To hear the pleading story;
   To Bethlehem they quickly came
   The glorious news to carry,
   And in the stall they found them all –
   Joseph, the Babe, and Mary.

8 The shepherds then return'd again
   To their own habitation,
   With joy of heart they did depart
   Now they have found salvation.
   Glory, they cry, to God on high,
   Who sent his Son to save us,
   This glorious morn the Savior's born,
   His name it is Christ Jesus.

The Southern Harmony, *1854, by courtesy of*
Hastings House, Publishers

COME AWAY TO THE SKIES

The Southern Harmony, *1854, arr. E. P.*

omitting D♯. It is effective that guitar play the tune as far as possible, bars 1-2, 4-5-6, 8-9

1 Come away to the skies, my beloved, arise
   And rejoice in the day thou wast born;
   On this festival day come exulting away,
   And with singing to Zion return.

2 Now with singing and praise let us spend all our days
   By our heavenly Father bestówed;
   While his grace we receive from his bounty, and live
   To the honor and glory of God.

The Southern Harmony, *1854, by courtesy of*
Hastings House, Publishers

WATTS'S CRADLE SONG

Tennessee, arr. E. P.

Gentle and smooth
Descant hummed, or instrumental con 8va ad lib.

1 Hush! my dear, lie still and slum-ber;
2 Sleep, my babe; thy food and rai-ment

Ho — ly an-gels guard thy bed! Heaven-ly bless-ings
House and home, thy friends pro-vide; All with-out— thy

repeats | *last time*

with-out num-ber Gent-ly fall-ing on thy head.
care and pay-ment, All thy wants are well sup-plied.

*omitting D♯

4-part version

4 Soft and ea-sy is thy cra-dle; Coarse and hard thy
5 Lo, he slum-bers in his man-ger, Where the horn-èd

Sa-viour lay, When his birth-place was a__ sta-ble
ox-en fed; Peace, my dar-ling! here's no__ dan-ger;

repeats   *last time*

And his soft-est bed was hay.
Here's no ox a-   -near thy bed.

1 Hush! my dear,* lie still and slumber;
   Holy angels guard thy bed!
   Heavenly blessings without number
   Gently falling on thy head.

2 Sleep, my babe; thy food and
      raiment,
   House and home, thy friends
      provide;
   All without thy care and payment,
   All thy wants are well supplied.

3 How much better thou'rt attended
   Than the Son of God could be
   When from heaven he descended
   And became a child like thee.

4 Soft and easy is thy cradle;
   Coarse and hard thy Saviour lay,
   When his birthplace was a stable
   And his softest bed was hay.

5 Lo, he slumbers in his manger,
   Where the hornèd oxen fed;
   Peace, my darling! here's no
      danger;
   Here's no ox a-near thy bed.

6 Mayst thou live to know and fear
      him,
   Trust and love him all thy days:
   Then go dwell for ever near him,
   See his face and sing his praise.

* *American version 'babe'*

Isaac Watts, 1674–1748

44

5 WATTS'S CRADLE SONG (SECOND TUNE)

American traditional, arr. E. P.

1 Hush! my babe, lie
Heaven - ly bless - ings

still and slum - ber; Ho - ly
with - out num - ber Gent - ly

an - gels guard thy bed!
fall - ing on thy head.

Instrumental / wordless *

3 How much__ bet - ter
When from__ hea - ven

thou'rt at - tend - ed Than the__
he de - scend - ed And be -

Son of God__ could__ be
-came a child__ like__ thee.

*trad. Scottish lullaby tune 'O can ye sew cushions'.

SHEPHERDS, REJOICE

The Social Harp, *John G. McCurry, 1868, arr. E. P.*

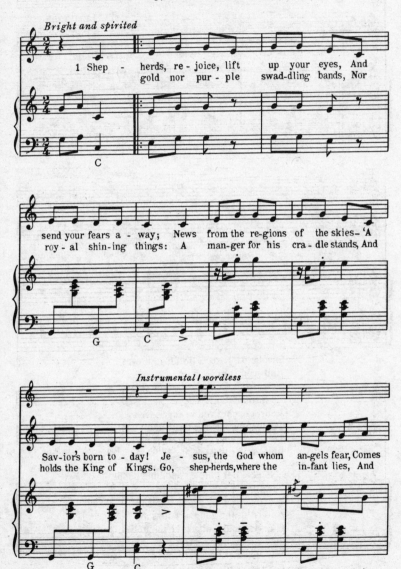

Bright and spirited

1 Shep - herds, re - joice, lift up your eyes, And send your fears a - way; News from the re-gions of the skies— 'A Sav-ior's born to - day! Je - sus, the God whom an-gels fear, Comes

gold nor pur - ple swad-dling bands, Nor roy - al shin-ing things: A man-ger for his cra - dle stands, And holds the King of Kings. Go, shep-herds, where the in-fant lies, And

Instrumental / wordless

down to dwell with you! To-day he makes his
see his hum-ble throne; With tears of joy in

en-trance here, But not as mon-archs do. 2 'No
all your eyes, Go, shep-herds, Kiss the Son.'

repeats *last time*

1 Shepherds, rejoice, lift up your eyes,
   And send your fears away;
   News from the regions of the skies –
   'A Savior's born today!
   Jesus, the God whom angels fear,
   Comes down to dwell with you !'
   Today he makes his entrance here,
   But not as monarchs do.

2 'No gold nor purple swaddling bands,
   Nor royal shining things:
   A manger for his cradle stands,
   And holds the King of Kings.
   Go, shepherds, where the infant lies,
   And see his humble throne;
   With tears of joy in all your eyes,
   Go, shepherds, kiss the Son.'

3 Thus Gabriel sang, and straight around
   The heavenly armies throng;
   They tune their harps to lofty sound,
   And thus conclude the song:
   ' Glory to God that reigns above,
   Let peace surround the earth;
   Mortals shall know their maker's love
   At their Redeemer's birth.'

4 Lord! and shall angels have their songs
   And men no tunes to raise?
   Oh, may we lose our useless tongues,
   When they forget to praise.
   Glory to God that reigns above,
   That pitied us forlorn;
   We join to sing our maker's love,
   For there's a Savior born.

Isaac Watts, 1674-1748
A Collection of Spiritual Songs used at the Camp
Meetings and in the Great Revival in the United States
of America, 1817; The Social Harp, *1868*

7

AWAY IN A MANGER

Tune by William James Kirkpatrick, 1838–1921, arr. E. P.

1 A - way in a__ man - ger, no__ crib for a bed, The lit - tle Lord Je - sus laid__ down his sweet head; The__

2 The cat - tle are__ low - ing, the__ ba - by a - wakes, But lit - tle Lord Je - sus, no__ cry - ing he makes: I__

Guitar Key G

G   Am   D   G   A7   D

stars in the bright sky looked down where he lay, The
love thee, Lord Je - sus; look down from the sky, And

lit - tle Lord Je - sus a - sleep on the hay.
stay by my side un - til morn - ing is nigh.

1 Away in a manger, no crib for a bed,
  The little Lord Jesus laid down his sweet head;
  The stars in the bright sky looked down where he lay,
  The little Lord Jesus asleep on the hay.

2 The cattle are lowing, the baby awakes,
  But little Lord Jesus, no crying he makes:
  I love thee, Lord Jesus; look down from the sky,
  And stay by my side until morning is nigh.

3 Be near me, Lord Jesus; I ask thee to stay
  Close by me for ever, and love me, I pray;
  Bless all the dear children in thy tender care,
  And fit us for heaven to live with thee there.

Anon., American, 1885

51

8

AWAY IN A MANGER (SECOND TUNE)

Traditional Basque, arr. E. P.

Simple and flowing

1 A - way in a — man - ger, no — crib for a bed, The lit - tle Lord Je - sus laid — down his sweet

3 Be near me, Lord — Je - sus; I — ask thee to stay Close by me for e - ver, and — love me, I

head; The stars in the___ bright sky looked
pray; Bless all the dear___ chil - dren in___

down where he lay, The___ lit - tle Lord___
thy ten - der care, And___ fit us for___

Je - sus a - sleep on the hay.
hea - ven to live with thee there.

poco cresc.

dim.

repeats | last time

Em Am C Am Dm Em A

Instrumental / wordless

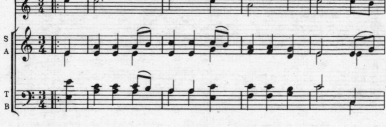

repeats　*last time*

RISE UP, SHEPHERD, AN' FOLLER

Christmas Plantation Song, arr. E. P.

1 There's a star in the East on Christ-mas morn, take good heed to the an - gel's words,

Rise up, shep-herd, an' fol-ler, { It 'll lead to the place where the You'll for- get your flocks, you'll for-

Sa - vior's born, — { *Rise up, shep-herd, an' fol-ler.* - get your herds, —

Guitar Key D

REFRAIN marked and rhythmical

Leave your sheep and leave your lambs,

Rise up, shep-herd, an' fol-ler; Leave your ewes an'

leave your rams, Rise up, shep-herd, an' fol-ler.

Fol - ler, fol - ler, Rise up, shep-herd, an'

fol-ler;   *Fol - ler the star of Beth - le - hem,__*

Rise up, shep-herd, an' fol-ler.

D   G

repeats   *last time*

Rise up, shep-herd, an' fol-ler.   *2 If you fol-ler.*

A7   D   D

1 There's a star in the East on Christmas morn,
     Rise up, shepherd, an' foller,
It'll lead to the place where the Savior's born,
     Rise up, shepherd, an' foller.
REFRAIN
     Leave your sheep and leave your lambs,
     Rise up, shepherd, an' foller;
     Leave your ewes an' leave your rams,
     Rise up, shepherd, an' foller.
     Foller, foller,
     Rise up, shepherd, an' foller;
     Foller the star of Bethlehem,
     Rise up, shepherd, an 'foller.

2 If you take good heed to the angel's words,
     Rise up, shepherd, an' foller,
You'll forget your flocks, you'll forget your herds,
     Rise up, shepherd, an' foller.
REFRAIN

Cherokee County, North Carolina, collected by John Jacob Niles, arr. E. P.

all good men for the new-born Ba-by!

Am   Em

Hum
mm

Lower voices prominent

3 And   at   that   pal - let   is__   a__   stone,
5 Be - side   that   bed   a   shrub tree grows, } Sing
6 Oh,   on   that   bed   a   young (Squire) sleeps,
                                        (Lord) } Sing

May,   Queen   May,   sing   Ma   -   ry! { On
                                            { Since
                                            { His

which   the   Vir - gin   did__   a - tone.
he   was   born   hit   blooms and__ blows. } Sing
wounds   are   sick,   and   see,__   he__ weeps.

all good men for the new-born Ba - by!

59

1 Down in yon forest be a hall,
   Sing May, Queen May, sing Mary!
   'Tis coverlidded over with purple and pall.
   Sing all good men for the new-born Baby!

2 Oh in that hall is a pallet bed:
   Sing May, Queen May, sing Mary!
   'Tis stained with blood like cardinal red.
   Sing all good men for the new-born Baby!

3 And at that pallet is a stone,
   Sing May, Queen May, sing Mary!
   On which the Virgin did atone.
   Sing all good men for the new-born Baby!

4 Under that hall is a gushing flood:
   Sing May, Queen May, sing Mary!
   From Christ's own side, 'tis water and blood.
   Sing all good men for the new-born Baby!

5 Beside that bed a shrub tree grows,
   Sing May, Queen May, sing Mary!
   Since he was born hit blooms and blows.
   Sing all good men for the new-born Baby!

6 Oh, on that bed a young { Squire / Lord } sleeps,
   Sing May, Queen May, sing Mary!
   His wounds are sick, and see, he weeps.
   Sing all good men for the new-born Baby!

7 Oh hail yon hall where none can sin,
   Sing May, Queen May, sing Mary!
   Cause hit's gold outside and silver within,
   Sing all good men for the new-born Baby!

In Ten Christmas Carols from the Appalachian Mountains, *coll. John Jacob Niles.*
Reprinted by permisson of G. Schirmer Inc.

THE BLESSINGS OF MARY

CARTHAGE, NORTH CAROLINA

Collected by Richard Chase, arr. E. P.

Moderate, strong

1 The ve-ry first bless - ing Ma - ry had, She
2 ve-ry next bless - ing Ma - ry had, She

mf

Guitar Key Em   Em

had the bless-ing of one;
had the bless-ing of two;
three;
etc.

To think that her son

Am   Em

Je - sus Could live a fa - ther's son, Could
Could read the Scrip-tures through, Could
Could set the sin - ner free, Could

1 The very first blessing Mary had,
  She had the blessing of one;
  To think that her son Jesus
  Could live a father's son,
  Could live a father's son
  Like the Manuel in glory;
    Father, Son, and the Holy Ghost,
    Through all eternity.

2 The very next blessing Mary had,
  She had the blessing of two;
  To think that her son Jesus
  Could read the Scriptures through,
  Could read the Scriptures through
  Like the Manuel in glory;
    Father, Son, and the Holy Ghost,
    Through all eternity.

3 . . . Could set the sinner free

4 . . . Could live for evermore

5 . . . Could bring the dead to live

6 . . . Could heal and cure the sick

7 . . . Could conquer Hell and Heaven

8 . . . Could make the crookèd straight

9 . . . Could turn the water to wine

10 . . . Could write without a pen

*Collected by Richard Chase, reprinted by courtesy of
the* Journal of American Folklore (*48, 1935*)

12 COME AND I WILL SING YOU

Collected by John Goss (1894-1953), in Oregon, arr. E. P.

Come to me dil-ly come dal-ly come dil-ly A - lone, ____ and e - ver shall re - main so. -main so.

poco marc.

last time Fine

B7* Emi

Group or voice 1

verses 2 to 12 Come and I will

Group or voice 2

sing you. What shall I sing you? I will sing you

*omitting D#

65

1 Come and I will sing you.
   What shall I sing you?
I will sing you one alone.
   What shall be the one alone?
One is one, and one alone.
   Come to me dilly come dally come dilly
   Alone, and ever shall remain so.

2 Come and I will sing you.
    What shall I sing you?
  I will sing you two of them.
    What shall be the two of them?
  Two are the Chrissymas babes in green,
  One is one, etc.

3 Three are the three that's in Bethlea,

4 Four's the gospellers at the door,

5 Five are the oxen standing by,

6 Six the six that never did mix,

7 Seven the shiners up in the sky,

8 Eight of them are the filly-shine white,

9 Nine of them's Aunt Mary Ann,

10 Ten are the ten commandîments,

11 'Leven eleven all gone to heaven,

12 Twelve's the followers all in a row,

Collected by John Goss, 1894–1953

13   CHILDREN, GO WHERE I SEND THEE

Negro Spiritual, arr. E. P.

Child - ren, go where I send thee!

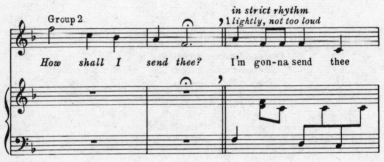

How shall I send thee? I'm gon-na send thee

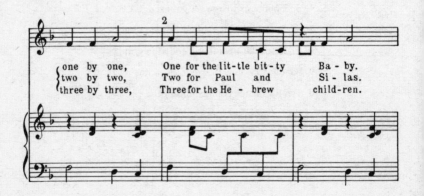

one by one, One for the lit-tle bit-ty Ba - by.
two by two, Two for Paul and Si - las.
three by three, Three for the He - brew child-ren.

All broadly

Born, born, Born in Beth-le-hem. Child-ren,

G   A7   D

Children, go where I send thee!
How shall I send thee?
1 I'm gonna send thee one by one,
One for the little bitty Baby.
Born, born,
Born in Bethlehem.

2 Two for Paul and Silas

3 Three for the Hebrew children

4 Four for the four that stood at the door

5 Five for the gospel preachers

6 Six for the six that never got fixed

7 Sev'n for the sev'n that never went to heav'n

8 Eight for the eight that stood at the gate

9 Nine for the nine that dressed so fine

10 Ten for the ten commandments

JOSEPH AND MARY

THE CHERRY TREE CAROL

Kentucky, transcribed and arranged E. P.

Jo-seph and Ma-ry was walk-ing, Was walk-ing one
5 Je - sus spoke a few words, A__ few words spoke
7 Jo - seph took__ Ma - ry All on his right
9 sixth of Ja - nu - a - ry My birth-day will

day, 'Here are ap - ples, here are cher-ries,'
he, 'Give my mo - ther some cher-ries, Bow
knee, 'What__ have I__ done, Lord?__ Have
be, The__ stars in__ the e - le-ments Will

Fine

Ma - ry did say. 3 Then
down, cher - ry tree! 8 Then
mer - cy on me.'
trem - ble with glee.'

Fine

1 Joseph was an old man,
   An old man was he,
   He married Virgin Mary,
   The Queen of Galilee.

2 As Joseph and Mary was walking,
   Was walking one day,
   'Here are apples, here are cherries,'
   Mary did say.

3 Then Mary said to Joseph,
   So meek and so mild,
   'Joseph gather me some cherries,
   For I am with child.'

4 Then Joseph flew in anger,
   In anger flew he,
   'Let the father of the baby
   Gather cherries for thee.'

5 Jesus spoke a few words,
   A few words spoke he,
   'Give my mother some cherries,
   Bow down, cherry tree!

6 'Bow down, cherry tree,
   Low down to the ground.'
   Mary gathered cherries,
   And Joseph stood around.

7 Then Joseph took Mary
   All on his right knee,
   'What have I done, Lord?
   Have mercy on me.'

8 Then Joseph took Mary
   All on his left knee,
   'Oh tell me, little Baby,
   When thy birthday will be.'

9 'The sixth of January
   My birthday will be,
   The stars in the elements
   Will tremble with glee.'

Transcribed from a field recording by John A. Lomax in the Archive of Folk Song, Library of Congress, of the singing of Jilson Setters (James W. Day) at Ashland, Kentucky, 28 June 1937

MARY HAD A BABY

ST HELENA ISLAND SPIRITUAL

Collected by N. G. J. Ballanta-Taylor, arr. E. P.

Group/Solo — All

1 Ma-ry had a ba-by, Aye, Lord,
2 Where did she lay him?

Ma-ry had a ba-by, Aye, my Lord, Ma-ry had a ba-by,
Where did she lay him? Where did she lay him?

Aye, Lord, The peo-ple keep a-com-in' and the train done gone.

Guitar Key G

G   G7   A7   D   G

1 Mary had a baby,
    Aye, Lord,
Mary had a baby,
    Aye, my Lord,
Mary had a baby,
    Aye, Lord,
The people keep a-comin' and the train done gone.

2 Where did she lay him?

3 Laid him in a manger

4 What did she name him?

5 Name him King Jesus

6 Who heard the singin'?

7 Shepherds heard the singin'

8 Star keep a-shining

9 Moving in the elements

10 Jesus went to Egypt

11 Traveled on a donkey

12 Angels went around him

Verse 1: coll. N. G. J. Ballanta-Taylor, St Helena Island Spirituals, *1925, reprinted by courtesy of Penn Community Services Inc., Frogmore, South Carolina. Verses 2–12: as sung extempore*

16

THE THREE KINGS OF ORIENT

EPIPHANY CAROL

John Henry Hopkins, jr., 1820 - 91, and arr. E. P.

*In dulci jubilo

roy - al beau - ty bright, West - ward

lead - ing, still pro - ceed - ing, Guide us

to thy per - fect light. *Fine*

Optional instrumental descant

MELCHIOR 2	Born a	King on	Beth - le - hem	plain,
GASPAR 3	Frank - in -	cense to	of - fer have	I;
BALTHAZAR 4	Myrrh is	mine; its	bit - ter per -	fume

Gold I bring, to crown him a - gain___
In - cense owns a De - i - ty nigh:
Breathes a life of ga - ther - ing gloom;

76

Heaven sings al - le - lu - ya,

Al - le - lu - ya___ the earth re - plies:

1 We three kings of Orient are;
  Bearing gifts we traverse afar
  Field and fountain, moor and mountain,
  Following yonder star:
    O star of wonder, star of night,
    Star with royal beauty bright,
    Westward leading, still proceeding,
    Guide us to thy perfect light.

MELCHIOR

2 Born a king on Bethlehem plain,
  Gold I bring, to crown him again –
  King for ever, ceasing never,
  Over us all to reign:

GASPAR

3 Frankincense to offer have I;
  Incense owns a Deity nigh:
  Prayer and praising, all men raising,
  Worship him, God most high:

BALTHAZAR

4 Myrrh is mine; its bitter perfume
  Breathes a life of gathering gloom;
  Sorrowing, sighing, bleeding, dying,
  Sealed in the stone-cold tomb:

ALL

5 Glorious now, behold him arise,
  King, and God, and sacrifice!
  Heaven sings alleluya,
  Alleluya the earth replies:

John Henry Hopkins, jr., 1820–91; written about 1837

78

17

GO TELL IT ON THE MOUNTAIN

Christmas Plantation Song, arr. E. P.

Guitar Key G

1 In the time of Da - vid, Some call him a king, And if a child is true born Lord Je - sus will hear him sing:

2 When I was a seek - er, I sought both night and day, I ask the Lord to help me, And he show me the way:

*To double bar (Refrain) single chords only on these beats

1 In the time of David,
  Some call him a king,
  And if a child is true born
  Lord Jesus will hear him sing:
    Go tell it on the mountain,
    Over the hills and everywhere,
    Go tell it on the mountain,
    That Jesus Christ is born.

2 When I was a seeker,
  I sought both night and day,
  I ask the Lord to help me,
  And he show me the way:

3 He made me a watchman
  Upon a city wall,
  And if I am a Christian
  I am the least of all:

  Religious Songs of the Negro as sung on the Plantations, *edited by Thomas P. Fenner, 1909*

18

CHARLES IVES'S CAROL

Charles Ives, 1874–1954

1 Lit - tle Star of Beth - le - hem!
2 O'er the cra - dle of a King,

Do__ we__ see thee now?
Hear__ the__ an-gels sing:

Do__ we see thee
In__ Ex-cel - sis

shin - ing__ o'er the tall trees?
glo - ri - a,__ Glo - - ria!__

Lit - tle Child of Beth - le-hem! Do__ we hear thee
From his fa - ther's home on high, Lo!__ for us he

in our hearts? Hear the an - gels sing - ing:
came to die; Hear the an - gels sing: Ve -

Peace__ on earth, good will to__ men!__
ni - te a - do - re - mus Do -

No - el!__
mi - num.__

83

19

CHARLES IVES'S CAROL

Charles Ives, 1874–1954

Adapted E. P. by permission of Theodore Presser Co. (Merion Music Inc.) from their publication © 1935 reprinted on the facing page

1 Little Star of Bethlehem!
Do we see thee now?
Do we see thee shining o'er the tall trees?
Little Child of Bethlehem!
Do we hear thee in our hearts?
Hear the angels singing:
Peace on earth, good will to men!
Noel!

2 O'er the cradle of a King,
Hear the angels sing:
In Excelsis gloria, Gloria!
From his father's home on high,
Lo! for us he came to die;
Hear the angels sing:
*Venite adoremus
Dominum.*

Author unknown

Tune Perseverance (adapted) in Wyeth's Repository of Sacred Music Part Second,
1820, arr. E. P.

1 I heard the
2 I thought how,

bells__ on Christ - mas Day Their old fa -
as__ the day__ had come, The bel - fries

mi - liar car - ols play, And
of all Christ - en - dom Had

mild and sweet the words_ re - peat *Of*
roll'd a - long th'un - bro - ken song. 4 *With*

peace on_ earth,_ good will_ to men.

1 I heard the bells on Christmas Day
Their old familiar carols play,
And mild and sweet the words
    repeat
Of peace on earth, good will to men.

2 I thought how, as the day had come,
The belfries of all Christendom
Had roll'd along th'unbroken song
Of peace on earth, good will to men.

3 And in despair I bow'd my head:
' There is no peace on earth,' I said,
' For hate is strong and mocks the
    song
Of peace on earth, good will to men.'

4 Then pealed the bells more loud and
    deep:
' God is not dead, nor doth he sleep:
The wrong shall fail, the right
    prevail,
*With peace on earth, good will to
    men.*'

Henry Wadsworth Longfellow, 1807–82

87

21

CHILD OF GOD
(THE LITTLE CRADLE ROCKS TONIGHT IN GLORY)
LOUISIANA AND GEORGIA

Collected by R. Emmett Kennedy (Mellows, 1925), arr. E. P.

who I am, _____ Tell him I'm a
night in glo - ry, The Christ child

Fine

child of God. 2 The
born in glo - ry.

1 If anybody ask you who I am,
  Who I am, who I am,
  If anybody ask you who I am;
  Tell him I'm a child of God.

2 The little cradle rocks tonight in glory,
  In glory, in glory,
  The little cradle rocks tonight in glory,
  The Christ child born in glory.

3 Peace on earth, Mary rock the cradle,
  Mary rock the cradle, Mary rock
    the cradle,
  Peace on earth, Mary rock the cradle,
  The Christ child born of glory.

4 The Christ child passing, singing
    softly,
  Singing softly, singing softly,
  The Christ child passing, singing
    softly,
  The Christ child born in glory.

5 Don't you hear the foot on the tree
    top,
  Foot on the tree top, foot on the tree
    top,
  Don't you hear the foot on the tree
    top,
  Soft like the south wind blow?

Verse 1: from Mellows *by R. Emmett Kennedy,*
reprinted by permission of Albert and Charles Boni Inc.
Verses 2–5: collected by Emma M. Backus, reprinted by
courtesy of the Journal of American Folklore *(xii, 1889)*

22

POOR LI'L JESUS

LOUISIANA

Collected by R. Emmett Kennedy (Mellows, 1925), arr. E. P.

2 Poor li'l Je - sus, *Hail, Lord,* They
4 Poor li'l Je - sus, *Hail, Lord,* They

Took him from a man - ger, *Hail, Lord,*
bound him with a hal - ter, *Hail, Lord,*

Took him from his mo - ther, *Hail, Lord, Ain' that a*
Whupped him up the moun-tain, *Hail, Lord, Ain' that a*

pi - ty   an' a   shame.

Am   B7   Em

1 Poor li'l Jesus,
    Hail, Lord,
  Child o' Mary,
    Hail, Lord,
  Born in a stable,
    Hail, Lord,
  Ain' that a pity an' a shame.

2 Poor li'l Jesus,
    Hail, Lord,
  Took him from a manger,
    Hail, Lord,
  Took him from his mother,
    Hail, Lord,
  Ain' that etc.

3 They give him to the Hebrew,
  They spit on his garment,

4 They bound him with a halter,
  Whupped him up the mountain,

5 They nailed him to the cross,
  They hung him with the robber,

6 Risen from the darkness,
  'scended into glory,

7 Meet me in the kingdom,
  Lead me to my Father,

From Mellows *by R. Emmett Kennedy, reprinted by permission of Albert and Charles Boni Inc.*

JESUS CHRIST THE APPLE TREE

Elizabeth Poston

things ex - cel: By faith I know, but

cresc.

ne'er can tell The glo - ry which I

now can see In Je - sus Christ the ap - ple tree.

4-Part or Unison acc.

3 For hap - pi - ness I long have sought, And
4 I'm wea - ry with my for - mer toil, Here

plea - sure dear - ly I have bought: For hap - pi - ness I
I will sit and rest a - while: I'm wea - ry with my

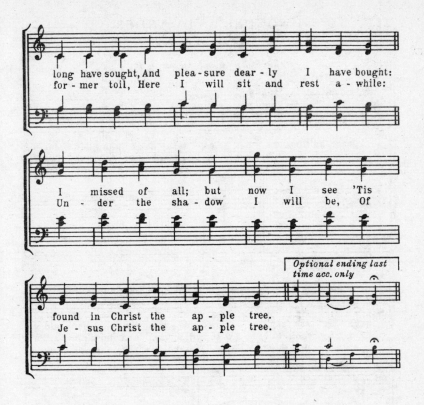

long have sought, And plea-sure dear-ly I have bought:
for-mer toil, Here I will sit and rest a-while:

I missed of all; but now I see 'Tis
Un - der the sha - dow I will be, Of

Optional ending last time acc. only

found in Christ the ap-ple tree.
Je - sus Christ the ap-ple tree.

1 The tree of life my soul hath seen,
Laden with fruit, and always green:
The trees of nature fruitless be
Compared with Christ the apple tree.

2 His beauty doth all things excel:
By faith I know, but ne'er can tell
The glory which I now can see
In Jesus Christ the apple tree.

3 For happiness I long have sought,
And pleasure dearly I have bought:
I missed of all; but now I see
'Tis found in Christ the apple tree.

4 I'm weary with my former toil,
Here I will sit and rest awhile:
Under the shadow I will be,
Of Jesus Christ the apple tree.

5 This fruit doth make my soul to thrive,
It keeps my dying faith alive;
Which makes my soul in haste to be
With Jesus Christ the apple tree.

Divine Hymns or Spiritual Songs, compiled by Joshua Smith, New Hampshire, 1784

95

24

I WONDER AS I WANDER

NORTH CAROLINA

Collected by John Niles, arr. E. P.

Simple, freely, as though improvising

1 unacc. ad lib. and 4 I won-der as I wan-der, out
2 When Ma-ry birthed Je-sus, 'twas
3 If Je-sus had want-ed for

un-der the sky, How Je-sus the Sa-vior did
in a cow's stall, With wise men and farm-ers and
a-ny wee thing, A star in the sky or a

come for to die For poor on-'ry peo-ple like
shep-herds and all. But high from the hea-vens a
bird on the wing, Or all of God's an-gels in

you and like I... I's s won-der as I wan-der, out
star's light did fall, And the pro-mise of a - ges it
heaven for to sing, He sure-ly could have had it, 'cause

Em   Am

repeats   *last time*

un-der the sky.
then did re - call.
he was the King.   un-der the sky.

Dm   Dm

1 I wonder as I wander, out under the sky,
  How Jesus the Savior did come for to die
  For poor on'ry people like you and like I . . .
  I wonder as I wander, out under the sky.

2 When Mary birthed Jesus, 'twas in a cow's stall,
  With wise men and farmers and shepherds and all.
  But high from the heavens a star's light did fall,
  And the promise of ages it then did recall.

3 If Jesus had wanted for any wee thing,
  A star in the sky or a bird on the wing,
  Or all of God's angels in heaven for to sing,
  He surely could have had it, 'cause he was the King.

4 I wonder as I wander, out under the sky,
  How Jesus the Savior did come for to die
  For poor on'ry people like you and like I . . .
  I wonder as I wander, out under the sky.

*Murphy, Cherokee County, North Carolina, in Songs of the Hill-Folk,
coll. John Jacob Niles, 1912. Reprinted by permission of G. Schirmer Inc.*

25

O LITTLE TOWN OF BETHLEHEM

FOREST GREEN

English traditional tune, arr. E. P.

Guitar G
Key G

O lit - tle town of Beth - le - hem,
A - bove thy deep and dream - less sleep

How still we see thee lie!
The si - lent stars go by.

C   D   G

Yet in thy dark streets shin - eth

The e - ver - last - ing light; The

C   D

hopes and fears of all__ the__ years

Are met in__ thee to - night.

G

C   D   G

1 O little town of Bethlehem,
      How still we see thee lie!
   Above thy deep and dreamless sleep
      The silent stars go by.
   Yet in thy dark streets shineth
      The everlasting light;
   The hopes and fears of all the years
      Are met in thee tonight.

2 O morning stars, together
      Proclaim the holy birth,
   And praises sing to God the King,
      For peace to men on earth;
   For Christ is born of Mary;
      And, gathered all above,
   While mortals sleep, the angels keep
      Their watch of wondering love.

3 How silently, how silently,
      The wondrous gift is given!
   So God imparts to human hearts
      The blessings of his heaven.

No ear may hear his coming;
   But in this world of sin,
Where meek souls will receive him, still
   The dear Christ enters in.

4 Where children pure and happy
      Pray to the blessèd Child,
   Where misery cries out to thee,
      Son of the mother mild;
   Where charity stands watching
      And faith holds wide the door,
   The dark night wakes, the glory breaks,
      And Christmas comes once more.

5 O holy Child of Bethlehem,
      Descend to us, we pray;
   Cast out our sin, and enter in,
      Be born in us today.
   We hear the Christmas Angels
      The great glad tidings tell:
   O come to us, abide with us,
      Our Lord Emmanuel.

Bishop Phillips Brooks (U.S.A.), 1835–93

99

26

JUDA'S LAND

APPALACHIAN CAROL

ed. and arr. E. P.

Slow and spacious

1 It was in Ju-da's land By
2 'Twas by his moth-er's hand He was

mp

Guitar Key E — E

God's al-might-y hand That Je-sus Christ was born in the
wrapped in swad-dling band And in a man-ger laid in the

B7 — E CHORUS
Louder

val - ley, val - ley, —

val - ley. —
val - ley. —

In the val-ley, — *In the*

E — A

val - ley, ____ That Je - sus Christ was
And in a man - ger

born ___ in the val - ley. _____
laid ___ in the val - ley. _____

E A E

A B7 E

Fine

1 It was in Juda's land
   By God's almighty hand
   That Jesus Christ was born in the valley.

   CHORUS
   In the valley,
   In the valley,
   That Jesus Christ was born in the valley.

2 'Twas by his mother's hand
   He was wrapped in swaddling band
   And in a manger laid in the valley.

   CHORUS
   In the valley,
   In the valley,
   And in a manger laid in the valley.

Appalachian carol by permission of Berea College, Berea, Kentucky

27

JESUS BORN IN BETHLEHEM
('SONG OF JESUS')

North Carolina, collected by Frank C. Brown, 1870–1943, arr. E. P.

lay.   And   in   a man-ger lay,   And
in   a man-ger lay;   Je - sus born in
Beth - le-hem And   in   a man-ger   lay.

1 Jesus born in Bethlehem,
   Jesus born in Bethlehem,
   Jesus born in Bethlehem,
     And in a manger lay.
   And in a manger lay,
   And in a manger lay;
   Jesus born in Bethlehem
     And in a manger lay.

2 His people crucified him *(3 times)*
     And nailed him on the cross,
   And nailed him on the cross, *(twice)*
   His people crucified him
     And nailed him on the cross.

3 Joseph begged his body *(3 times)*
     And laid it in the tomb,
   And laid it in the tomb, *(twice)*
   Joseph begged his body
     And laid it in the tomb.

4 The tomb it would not hold it;
                   (3 times)
   He burst the bars of death.
   He burst the bars of death, *(twice)*
   The tomb it would not hold it;
   He burst the bars of death.

5 Mary came weeping *(3 times)*
     About her lovely Lord.
   About her lovely Lord, *(twice)*
   Mary came weeping
     About her lovely Lord.

6 'What's the matter, Mary?' *(3 times)*
     'They've stole my Lord away.'
   'They've stole my Lord away, *(twice)*
   'What's the matter, Mary?'
     'They've stole my Lord away.'

7 They found Jesus living, *(3 times)*
     Alive forever more.
   Alive forever more, *(twice)*
   They found Jesus living,
     Alive forever more.

8 He ascended to his father,
   Ascended to his father *(twice)*
     To reign with him on high.
   To reign with him on high, *(twice)*
   Ascended to his father,
     To reign with him on high.

From the Frank C. Brown Collection of North Carolina Folklore, *Duke University Press, Durham, North Carolina. Reprinted by permission*

28

LULLE LULLAY

TENNESSEE

Collected by John Jacob Niles, arr. E. P.

Gently flowing, expressively with the rise and fall

1 Lul - lay,— thou ti - ny lit - tle child, Bye-bye, lul - le,— lul - lay;— Lul - lay, thou ti - ny lit - tle child, Bye - bye, *lul - le,— lul - lay.—* 2 Oh

3 -rod— the King, in his— rag -ing, Charg-ed— he hath this day— His sold -iers in— their strength and might All chil - dren young to slay.— 4 Then

Guitar Key Emi · Emi · D · Emi · G · Emi · D · Emi

sis - ters two, how may we do To per - se - vere this
woe is me, poor child, for thee, And e - ver mourn and

day? To this poor youngling *(child-ling)* for whom we sing Bye-
say, For at thy part - ing nor say - nor sing Bye-

bye, lul-le, lul - lay. 3 He-

repeats *last time*

106

1 Lullay, thou tiny little child,
  Bye-bye, lulle, lullay;
  Lullay, thou tiny little child,
  Bye-bye, lulle, lullay.

2 Oh sisters two, how may we do
  To persevere this day?
  To this poor $\left\{\begin{array}{l}\text{childling} \\ \text{youngling}\end{array}\right\}$ for whom we sing
  Bye-bye, lulle, lullay.

3 Herod, the King, in his raging,
  Chargèd he hath this day
  His soldiers in their strength and might
  All children young to slay.

4 Then woe is me, poor child, for thee,
  And ever mourn and say,
  For at thy parting nor say nor sing
  Bye-bye, lulle, lullay.

5 And when the stars ingather do,
  In their far venture stay,
  Then smile as dreaming, little one,
  Bye-bye, lulle, lullay.

*Recorded at Gatlinburg, Tennessee, 16 June 1934 from
' the old lady with the gray hat ', by John Jacob Niles.
In* Ten Christmas Carols from the Appalachian
Mountains, *1935. Reprinted by permission of G.
Schirmer Inc.*

29

SHEPHERDS IN JUDEA

Compiled by (attributed to) Jeremiah Ingalls, 1764–1828, arr. E. P.

Fairly fast, brightly

1 As shep-herds in Jew-ry were guard-ing their
2 Though A-dam the first in re-bel-lion was

sheep, Pro-mis-c'ous-ly seat-ed, es-trang-ed from sleep, An
found, For-bid-den to tar-ry in hal-low-ed ground; Yet

an-gel from hea-ven pre-sent-ed to view, And
A-dam the se-cond ap-pears to re-trieve The

REFRAIN 1-2

thus he ac-cost-ed the trem-bl-ing few: Dis-
loss you sus-tain'd by the dev-il and Eve. Then

-pel all your sor-rows and ba-nish your fears, For__
shep-herds, be tran-quil, this in-stant a-rise, Go__

Je-sus your Sav-ior in Jew-ry ap-pears, Dis-
vis-it your Sav-ior and see where he lies, Then

-pel all your sor-rows and ba-nish your fears, For
shep-herds, be tran-quil, this in-stant a-rise, Go

Je - sus your Sav - ior in__ Jew - ry ap - pears.
vis - it your Sav - ior and__ see where he lies.

A7   D

1   As shepherds in Jewry were guarding their sheep,
    Promisc'ously seated, estrangèd from sleep,
    An angel from heaven presented to view,
    And thus he accosted the trem-bl-ing few:
    REFRAIN 1
    Dispel all your sorrows and banish your fears,   *(twice)*
    For Jesus your Savior in Jewry appears.

2   Though Adam the first in rebellion was found,
    Forbidden to tarry in hallowèd ground;
    Yet Adam the second appears to retrieve
    The loss you sustain'd by the devil and Eve.
    REFRAIN 2
    Then shepherds, be tranquil, this instant arise,   *(twice)*
    Go visit your Savior and see where he lies.

3   A token I leave you, whereby you may find
    This heavenly stranger, this friend to mankind:
    A manger his cradle, a stall his abode,
    The oxen are near him and blow on your God.
    REFRAIN 3
    Then shepherds, be humble, be meek and be low,   *(twice)*
    For Jesus your Savior's abundantly so.

4   This wonderful story scarce reachèd the ear,
    When thousands of angels in glory appear,
    They join in the concert, and this was the theme:
    All glory to God, and good will towards men.
    REFRAIN 4
    Then shepherds, go join your glad voice to the choir,   *(twice)*
    And catch a few sparks of celestial fire.

5 Hosanna! the angels in ecstasy cry,
   Hosanna! the wandering shepherds reply;
   Salvation, redemption are center'd in one,
   All glory to God for the birth of his Son.
   REFRAIN 5
   Then shepherds, adore, we commend you to God, } *(twice)*
   Go visit the Son in his humble abode.

6 To Bethlehem city the shepherds repair'd,
   For full confirmation of what they had heard;
   They enter'd the stable, with aspect so mild,
   And there they beheld the Mother and Child.
   REFRAIN 6
   Then make proclamation, divulge it abroad, } *(twice)*
   That both Jews and Gentiles may hear of the Lord,

The Christian Harmony; or Songster's Companion,
*compiled by Jeremiah Ingalls, Exeter, New Hartford,
1805. Printed in* Down-East Spirituals *by George
Pullen Jackson, 2nd edition, 1953. J. J. Augustin
Incorporated Publisher. Reprinted by permission*

30

HEAV'N BELL-A RING

South Carolina, arr. E. P.

1 Say Christ-mas come but once a year,
2 My Lord, my Lord, what shall I do?
3 You look to the Lord with a ten-der heart,

And-a heav'n bell-a ring and praise God.

Christ-mas come but once a year,
Lord, my Lord, what shall I do?
look to the Lord with a ten-der heart,

And-a heav'n bell-a ring and praise God.

Guitar Key G

The C-D figure goes well with chime bars.

1 Say Christmas come but once a year,
   And-a heav'n bell-a ring and praise God.
   Say Christmas come but once a year,
   And-a heav'n bell-a ring and praise God.

2 My Lord, my Lord, what shall I do?

3 You look to the Lord with a tender heart,

4 He cast out none that come by faith.
   repeat 1 *ad lib*

Slave Songs of the United States, *1867*

31

WHAT YOU GONNA CALL YO' PRETTY LITTLE BABY?

Negro spiritual, arr. E. P.

Steady, rather slow, strongly rhythmical

What you gon-na call yo' pret-ty lit-tle ba - by,

What you gon-na call yo' pret-ty lit-tle ba - by, What you gon-na call yo'

pret-ty lit-tle ba - by? *Born, born in Beth-le - hem.*

mf non leg.   *mp*

Guitar Key Em   Em   G   Em   A   B7   Em

1 Some say one thing, I'll say Im-man-uel.
2 Some call him one thing, I'll call him Je-sus.
3 Sweet lit-tle ba - by, born in a man - ger.

Born, born in Beth - le - hem.

1 What you gonna call yo' pretty little baby,
  What you gonna call yo' pretty little baby,
  What you gonna call yo' pretty little baby?
  Born, born in Bethlehem.
  Some say one thing, I'll say Immanuel.
  Born, born in Bethlehem.

2 What you gonna call yo' pretty little baby, *etc.*
  Some call him one thing, I'll call him Jesus.
  Born, born in Bethlehem.

3 What you gonna call yo' pretty little baby, *etc.*
  Sweet little baby, born in a manger.
  Born, born in Bethlehem.

32

OH, MARY AND THE BABY, SWEET LAMB

Texas, transcribed and arr. E. P.

1,4,6 Oh, Ma-ry and the Ba-by,
2 It's a ho-ly Ba-by, } sweet Lamb,
3 I love that Ba-by,
5 It's a God-sent Ba-by,

Guitar Key Em   Em

Oh, Ma-ry and the Ba-by,
It's a ho-ly Ba-by, } sweet Lamb,
I love that Ba-by,
It's a God-sent Ba-by,

1 Oh, Mary and the Baby, sweet Lamb,
   Oh, Mary and the Baby, sweet Lamb,
   Oh, Mary and the Baby, sweet Lamb,
   Oh, Mary and the Baby, sweet Lamb.

2 It's a holy Baby, sweet Lamb,
   It's a holy Baby, sweet Lamb,
   It's a holy Baby, sweet Lamb,
   Oh, Mary and the Baby, sweet Lamb.

3 I love that Baby, sweet Lamb,   *(3 times)*
   Oh, Mary and the Baby, sweet Lamb.

4 Oh, Mary and the Baby, sweet Lamb   *(4 times)*

5 It's a God-sent Baby, sweet Lamb,   *(3 times)*
   Oh, Mary and the Baby, sweet Lamb.

6 Oh, Mary and the Baby, sweet Lamb   *(4 times)*

Transcribed from a field recording by John A. Lomax in the Archive of Folk Song, Library of Congress, of the singing of Ella Mitchell and Velma Wright at Lubbock, Texas, 19 January 1937

33

LAST MONTH O' THE YEAR
WHEN WAS JESUS BORN?

Christmas spiritual, arr. E. P.

born? *Well, it was last month o' the year.*

last month o' the

C   G

Guitar rest _ _ _ _ _ _   Play voice tune _
Solo *poco f*   2   All

When was Je-sus born? *Well, it was last month o' the*

year.

G

year.   Ja - nu-ar-y?   Feb-ru-a-ry?

March, A-pril, May? June, a-Ju - ly?

August, Sep - tem-ber, Oc - to-ber, No - a-vem - ber? The

twen-ty-fifth day o' De - a-cem-ber, *the last month o' the year.*

Fine

Quietly

Now he was born of the Vir-gin Ma-ry, Wrapp'd up in the swad-dlin', Laid in the man-ger, The

O tell me, when was Jesus born?
  Well, it was last month o' the year.
When was Jesus born?
  Well, it was last month o' the year. { *(twice)*
        January? February? March, April, May?
        June, a-July? August, September, October, No-a-vember?
        The twenty-fifth day o' De-a-cember,
          the last month o' the year.
Now he was born of the Virgin Mary,
Wrapp'd up in the swaddlin',
Laid in the manger,
        The twenty-fifth day o' De-a-cember,
          the last month o' the year.

34

O MARY, WHERE IS YOUR BABY?

LOUISIANA

Collected by R. Emmett Kennedy (Mellows, 1925), arr. E. P.

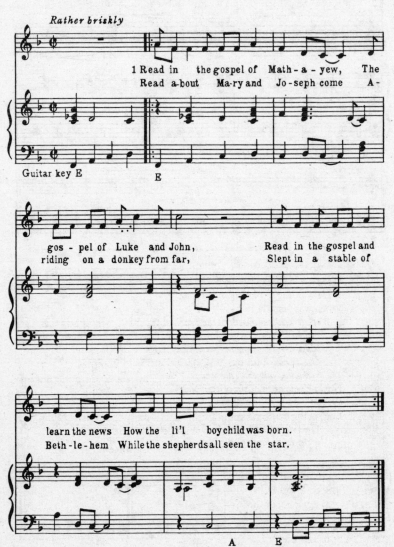

Rather briskly

Guitar key E

E

1 Read in the gospel of Math-a-yew, The
Read a-bout Ma-ry and Jo-seph come A-

gos-pel of Luke and John, Read in the gospel and
riding on a donkey from far, Slept in a stable of

learn the news How the li'l boy child was born.
Beth-le-hem While the shepherds all seen the star.

A   E

REFRAIN
Instrumental

O _____ Ma - ry, Where is your

E

ba - by? They done took him from a man-ger And

car-ried him to the throne.   throne.

B7   E   E

1 Read in the gospel of Mathayew,
  The gospel of Luke and John,
  Read in the gospel and learn the news
  How the li'l boy child was born.
  Read about Mary and Joseph come
  A-riding on a donkey from far,
  Slept in a stable of Bethlehem
  While the shepherds all seen the star.

  > REFRAIN
  > *O Mary,*
  > *Where is your baby?*
  > *They done took him from a manger*
  > *And carried him to the throne.*

2 Read about the elders and the Hebrew priest,
  A-preaching in the tabernacle hall;
  Standing in a wonder at the words they heard
  From a li'l boy child so small.
  'O li'l boy, how old you is?
  Tell me if you let it be told.
  O li'l boy, how old you is?'
  'I ain't but twelve years old.'

From Mellows *by R. Emmett Kennedy, reprinted by permission of Albert and Charles Boni Inc.*

35

VIRGIN MARY, MEEK AND MILD

Kentucky, collected by John Jacob Niles, arr. E. P.

1 Vir - gin Ma - ry, meek and mild,
2 Pet - er, Pet-er, Pet-er, Pet-er, run get your keys,
3 Ga - briel, Ga - briel, oil your horn,

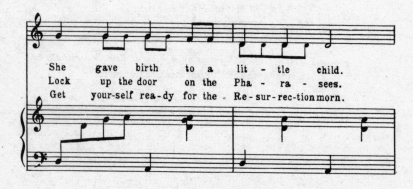

She gave birth to a lit - tle child.
Lock up the door on the Pha - ra - sees.
Get your-self rea-dy for the Re - sur - rec-tion morn.

Great-day com-in', Com - in' soon. Ne-ver been there be -

1 Virgin Mary, meek and mild,
  She gave birth to a little child.
      Great day comin',
      Comin' soon.
      Never been there before,*
      Never been there before.

2 Peter, Peter, Peter, Peter, run get your keys,
  Lock up the door on the Pharasees.

3 Gabriel, Gabriel, oil your horn,
  Get yourself ready for the Resurrection morn.

Recorded in Burnside, Kentucky, summer 1912,
by John Jacob Niles. In Seven Negro Exaltations.
Reprinted by permission of G. Schirmer Inc.

* *da befo'.*

36

SUNNY BANK
(CHRISTMAS DAY IN THE MORNING)

Virginia, collected by Winston Wilkinson, arr. E. P.

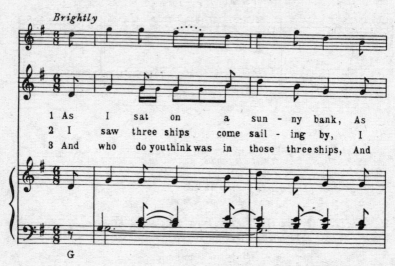

1 As I sat on a sun - ny bank, As
2 I saw three ships come sail - ing by, I
3 And who do you think was in those three ships, And

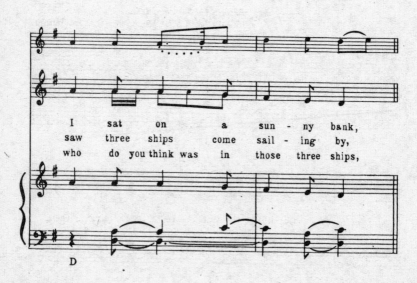

I sat on a sun - ny bank,
saw three ships come sail - ing by,
who do you think was in those three ships,

As I sat on a sun - ny bank,
I saw three ships come sail - ing by, } On
And who do you think was in those three ships, But

G

Fine

Christ - mas Day in the morn - ing.
3 Jo - seph and his fair la - dy.

D   G

Others whistle the tune

4 Then he did whis - tle and she did sing, Then

Melody

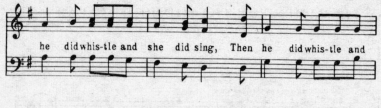

he did whis-tle and she did sing, Then he did whis-tle and

she did sing, On Christ - mas Day in the morn - ing.

1 As I sat on a sunny bank,
 As I sat on a sunny bank,
 As I sat on a sunny bank,
 On Christmas Day in the morning.

2 I saw three ships come sailing by,   *(3 times)*
 On Christmas Day in the morning.

3 And who do you think was in those three ships, *(3 times)*
 But Joseph and his fair lady.

4 Then he did whistle and she did sing,   *(3 times)*
 On Christmas Day in the morning.

5 And all the bells on earth did ring,   *(3 times)*

6 And all the angels in heaven did sing,   *(3 times)*

7 For joy that Christ is born our King,   *(3 times)*

*University of Virginia (Manuscript) Collection of
Folk-Music, from the singing of Arthur Morris,
Charlottesville, Virginia, 1936. Reprinted in Down-
East Spirituals by George Pullen Jackson. J. J.
Augustin Incorporated Publisher.
Reprinted by permission*

37 IT CAME UPON THE MIDNIGHT CLEAR
NOEL

English traditional, harm. Arthur Sullivan, 1842–1900, descant E. P.

Moderate
Vocal and instrumental

1 It__ came up - on the__ mid - night clear, That glo-rious song of old, From an-gels bend - ing near the earth To__ touch their harps of gold:

'Peace on the earth, good will to men, From
heav'n's all - gra-cious King!' The world in so - lemn
still - ness lay To— hear the an-gels sing.

1 It came upon the midnight clear,
   That glorious song of old,
From angels bending near the earth
   To touch their harps of gold:
'Peace on the earth, good will to men,
   From heav'n's all-gracious King!'
The world in solemn stillness lay
   To hear the angels sing.

2 Still through the cloven skies they come,
   With peaceful wings unfurled;
And still their heavenly music floats
   O'er all the weary world;
Above its sad and lowly plains
   They bend on hovering wing:
And ever o'er its Babel sounds
   The blessèd angels sing.

3 Yet with the woes of sin and strife,
   The world has suffered long;
Beneath the angel-strain have rolled
   Two thousand years of wrong;
And man, at war with man, hears not
   The love-song which they bring;
O hush the noise, ye men of strife,
   And hear the angels sing.

4 And ye, beneath life's crushing load,
   Whose forms are bending low,
Who toil along the climbing way
   With painful steps and slow,
Take heart, for comfort, love, and hope
   Come swiftly on the wing;
O rest beside the weary road,
   And hear the angels sing.

5 For lo, the days are hastening on,
   That prophets knew of old,
And with the ever-circling years
   Comes round the day foretold.
May peace on earth in every land
   Its joy and healing bring,
And the whole world send back the song
   Which now the angels sing.

E. H. Sears, 1810–76 (the last verse adapted)

SISTER MARY HAD-A BUT ONE CHILD

Christmas spiritual, arr. E. P.

Rather quicker, lively

O three wise men to Je-ru-sa-lem came, They
He-rod's heart was trou-bled, He

tra-velled ve-ry far, They said 'Where is he, born
mar-velled but his face was grim; He said 'Tell me where the

Emi

King of the Jews, For we have seen His star?' King
child may be found, I'll go and wor-ship him, I'll

Ami   G

go and wor - ship him,   I'll go and wor - ship him.'

Ami   G

2 An an-gel ap-peared to_ Jo-seph,_ And gave him this - a com-

mand,   'A - rise ye, take-a   your   wife and child, Go

flee in-to E - gypt's land.__ For yon-der comes old

He - rod,__   A wick-ed man_ and bold, He's

slay-ing all_ the chil-lun__ From six to eight - a days

old,   From   six to eight - a days old?

136

Sister Mary had-a but one child,
Born in Bethlehem,
And every time the baby cried,
She-a rocked him in the weary land,
She-a rocked him in the weary land.

1 O three wise men to Jerusalem came,
They travelled very far,
They said, ' Where is he, born King of the Jews,
For we have seen his star?'
King Herod's heart was troubled,
He marvelled but his face was grim;
He said, ' Tell me where the child may be found,
I'll go and worship him.' *(twice)*
REFRAIN

2 An angel appeared to Joseph,
And gave him this-a command,
' Arise ye, take-a your wife and child,
Go flee into Egypt's land.
For yonder comes old Herod,
A wicked man and bold,
He's slaying all the chillun
From six to eight-a days old.' *(twice)*
REFRAIN

39 SWEEP, SWEEP AND CLEANSE YOUR FLOOR

Shaker ritual song, arr. E. P.

Sweep, sweep and cleanse your floor,
Mo-ther's stand-ing at the door, She'll give us good and
pre-cious wheat With which there is no chaff nor cheat.
I'll sow my wheat up - on the ground That's

This song was probably sung in slow tempo. In our own time, it may be taken in Polka tempo ♩ = approx. 64

Sweep, sweep and cleanse your floor,
Mother's standing at the door,
She'll give us good and precious wheat
With which there is no chaff nor cheat.
I'll sow my wheat upon the ground
That's plough'd and till'd and where is found
A faithful laborer of the field,
That it a rich increase may yield.

New Lebanon Hymnal, *attrib. Eleanor Potter, 1839,
from* The Gift to be Simple *by Edward Andrews.
Dover Publications, Inc., New York. Reprinted through
the permission of the publisher*

* *From here to the end of the verse the original stays in the lower octave, here placed in
the upper*

SAINT STEPHEN AND HEROD

VERMONT

Collected by Helen Hartness Flanders, arr. E. P.

1 Saint Ste-phen was a serv-ing-man In He-rod's roy-al hall; ____ He serv-ed him with meat and wine That doth to Kings be-fall. ____

2 He was serv-ing him with meat, one day, With a boar's head in his hand, ____ When he saw a star come from the East And o-ver Beth-lehem stand. ____

1 Saint Stephen was a serving-man
   In Herod's royal hall;
   He servèd him with meat and wine
   That doth to kings befall.

2 He was serving him with meat, one day,
   With a boar's head in his hand,
   When he saw a star come from the East
   And over Bethlehem stand.

3 Saint Stephen was a righteous man
   And in his faith was bold.
   He was waiting for the birth of Christ
   As by the prophets told.

4 He cast the boar's head on the floor
   And let the server fall;
   He said, ' Behold a child is born
   That is better than we all.'

5 Then quickly he went to Herod's room
   And unto him did say,
   ' I am leaving thee, King Herod,
   And will proclaim thy wicked ways.'

Used by permission of the copyright owner, Helen Hartness Flanders, as published in Ballads Migrant in New England © *1953, 1968, pp. 217–18*

BABY BORN TODAY
MOTHER MARY, WHAT IS THE MATTER?

Southern traditional Christmas Eve Watch-night 'shout'
Collected by John Goss, 1894-1953, arr. E. P.

At a moderate speed, declaiming flexibly

Solo-Group

1 Mo-ther Ma-ry, what is the mat-ter?

All

Oh, Je-ru-s'lem in the morn — ing!

Solo/Group

2 Fa-ther Jo-seph, what is the mat-ter?

All

Oh, Je-ru-s'lem in the morn — ing! 3 A

Guitar Key D   D   A7   D

1 Mother Mary, what is the matter?
   Oh, Jerus'lem in the morning!

2 Father Joseph, what is the matter?
   Oh, Jerus'lem in the morning!

3 A baby born today,
   Oh, etc.

4 Born in the manger,

5 They wrapped in swaddling clothes,

6 Stall was his cradle,

7 Born in Bethlehem,

8 Born in the manger,

9 Jerus'lem, Oh, Jerus'lem,

10 Baby born today,
   Oh, Jerus'lem in the morning!

*Verses 1 and 2: from the singing of Ella Garrett c. 1939.
Verses 1–10: from* Folk-Songs of America *by Robert
W. Gordon.* © *1927–8 by The New York Times
Company. Reprinted by permission*

WASN'T THAT A MIGHTY DAY

SOUTH CAROLINA AND TENNESSEE

Collected by N. G. J. Ballanta-Taylor, arr. E. P.*

Rather fast, strongly rhythmical REFRAIN

Was-n't that a might-y day,

Hal-le - lu,_ Hal-le - lu,_ Was-n't that a might-y

day, When Je - sus Christ was born.

* St Helena Island Spirituals, *1925. Reprinted by courtesy of Penn Community Services Inc., Frogmore, South Carolina*

Well, Je-sus was a ba-by, A-ly-ing at Ma-ry's arm, Ly-ing in the sta-ble at Beth-le-hem, The beasts they keep-a him warm.

D   G

This song is effective sung softly with great intensity

REFRAIN
Wasn't that a mighty day,
  Hallelu, Hallelu,
Wasn't that a mighty day
When Jesus Christ was born.
Well, Jesus was a baby,
A-lying at Mary's arm,
Lying in the stable at Bethlehem,
The beasts they keep-a him warm.
REFRAIN

'Some Negro Folk Songs from Tennessee' *by Anna Kranz Odum, reprinted by courtesy of the* Journal of American Folklore (*xxvii, 264, 1924*)

43 THE TWELVE DAYS OF CHRISTMAS

traditional American forfeit song
Florida, collected by Alton C. Morris, transcribed and arr. E. P.

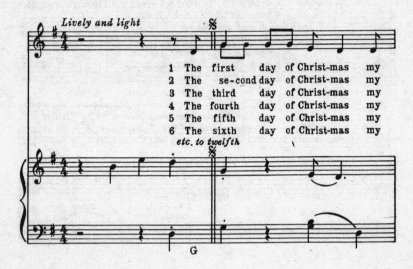

1 The first day of Christ-mas my
2 The se-cond day of Christ-mas my
3 The third day of Christ-mas my
4 The fourth day of Christ-mas my
5 The fifth day of Christ-mas my
6 The sixth day of Christ-mas my
etc. to twelfth

true-love sent to_ me   1 A(*to*1)   6 Six geese a-lay-ing (*to*5)
true-love sent to_ me   (*to*2)   7 Seven swans a-swim-ming(*to*6)
true-love sent to_ me   (*to*3)   8 Eight maids a-danc-ing, (*to*7)
true-love sent to_ me   (*to*4)   9 Nine hares a-run-ning, (*to*8)
true-love sent to_ me   (*to*5) 10 Ten hounds a-hunt-ing, (*to*9)
true-love sent to_ me   (*to*6) 11 Eleven lords a-leap-ing, (*to*10)
                                    12 Twelve bulls a-roar-ing, (*to*11)

1 The first day of Christmas my true-love sent to me
A partridge on a pear-tree.

2 The second day of Christmas my true-love sent to me
Two turtle doves,
A partridge on a pear-tree.

3 The third day of Christmas my true-love sent to me
Three French hens,
Two turtle doves,
A partridge on a pear-tree.

4 The fourth day of Christmas my true-love sent to me
Four colored birds,
Three French hens,
Two turtle doves,
A partridge on a pear-tree.

5 The fifth day of Christmas my true-love sent to me
Five gold rings,
Four colored birds
etc.

6 Six geese a-laying,

7 Seven swans a-swimming,

8 Eight maids a-dancing,

9 Nine hares a-running,

10 Ten hounds a-hunting,

11 Eleven lords a-leaping,

12 Twelve bulls a-roaring,

Transcribed from a field recording by Alton C. Morris in the Archive of Folk Song, Library of Congress, of the singing of Mrs Susie Morrison at Gainesville, Florida, 19 April 1937

INDEX OF TITLES, FIRST LINES
AND CHORUSES

INDEX OF AUTHORS, COLLECTORS, COMPILERS, COMPOSERS AND ARRANGERS

MORE ABOUT PENGUINS
AND PELICANS

Penguinews, which appears every month, contains details of all the new books issued by Penguins as they are published. From time to time it is supplemented by *Penguins in Print*, which is our complete list of almost 5,000 titles.

A specimen copy of *Penguinews* will be sent to you free on request. Please write to Dept EP, Penguin Books Ltd, Harmondsworth, Middlesex, for your copy.

In the U.S.A.: For a complete list of books available from Penguins in the United States write to Dept CS, Penguin Books, 625 Madison Avenue, New York, New York 10022.

In Canada: For a complete list of books available from Penguins in Canada write to Penguin Books Canada Ltd, 2801 John Street, Markham, Ontario LR3 1B4.

THE PELICAN HISTORY OF MUSIC

EDITED BY ALEC ROBERTSON AND DENIS STEVENS

The concert-goer and music-lover anxious to discover some of the hidden wealth of musical history will find in this series of three volumes an account of many kinds of music: primitive and non-Western, liturgical, medieval, renaissance, baroque, classical, romantic, and modern. Although there is some technical analysis, the authors and editors have concentrated on fitting music into its proper frame, whether ecclesiastical, courtly, or popular.

Each musical epoch is discussed by an expert who considers the music at its face value, instead of thinking of it merely as a link in a chain of development ending in the music of Beethoven or Boulez. The reader can therefore come to understand musical trends and styles both within and without the normal orbit of concerts and opera, and will be able to enjoy unfamiliar music as well as the accepted classics.

A special feature of the first two volumes is the group of illustrations that have been chosen to set the scene rather than to illustrate any specific points in the text.

Volume 1: ANCIENT FORMS TO POLYPHONY
Volume 2: RENAISSANCE AND BAROQUE
Volume 3: CLASSICAL AND ROMANTIC

THE PENGUIN BOOK OF ENGLISH
MADRIGALS FOR FOUR VOICES

EDITED BY DENIS STEVENS

In compiling this collection of English madrigals Professor Denis
Stevens, who founded the Ambrosian Consort, has adopted an
entirely fresh style of presentation. Each madrigal is prefaced by a
fully edited version of the poem, with notes on features of special
interest in lyric or music. The music, which is set for four voices,
has been edited in a new way, too, so as to help singers to achieve a
finer balance and more perfect ensemble in this most subtle of
musical styles.

Also published

THE SECOND PENGUIN BOOK OF ENGLISH
MADRIGALS: FOR FIVE VOICES

EDITED BY DENIS STEVENS

This second book of English Madrigals contains twenty-one works
picked from the cream of the repertory for five voices. As in the
previous volume each madrigal has been edited and introduced,
with the modern amateur performer especially in mind, by Professor
Denis Stevens.

THE PENGUIN BOOK OF ENGLISH FOLK SONGS

EDITED BY RALPH VAUGHAN WILLIAMS
AND A. L. LLOYD

A classic collection of seventy of the rarer songs recovered from the counties of England by enthusiasts during this century and presented here by Dr Ralph Vaughan Williams and A. L. Lloyd with melodies and notes on their origins.

THE PENGUIN BOOK OF AMERICAN FOLK SONGS

ALAN LOMAX

North America has been the meeting place for a number of very diverse folksong styles, each one uprooted from its homeland and transported to the new world. Every linguistic minority in the American melting pot has preserved at least some fragments of its oral tradition.

Alan Lomax has made several song-hunting trips round the United States and in *The Penguin Book of American Folk Song* he has compiled and edited a large representative selection of songs with piano accompaniments arranged by Elizabeth Poston.

Sections of the book are devoted to Yankee Songs, Southern Mountain Songs, Lullabies and Reels, Spirituals and Work Songs, Western Songs, and Songs of Modern Times.

The companion to this volume:

THE PENGUIN BOOK OF CHRISTMAS CAROLS

ELIZABETH POSTON

This collection of fifty Christmas carols has been made by Elizabeth Poston, the well-known composer and folk-song expert. She herself has arranged the music for the carols, providing each with a simple vocal or instrumental descant. The carols included range from 'Hark, the Herald Angels' to folk carols culled from English, French, and Russian sources. Special care has been taken to translate the foreign carols into words that are a pleasure to sing.